PENGUIN BOOKS

# YOU ARE A BADASS AT
# MAKING MONEY

Jen Sincero is a world-renowned author, success coach, and motivational speaker who's spent over a decade helping countless people transform their personal and professional lives.

## ALSO BY JEN SINCERO

*You Are a Badass: How to Stop Doubting Your Greatness
and Start Living an Awesome Life*

*The Straight Girl's Guide to Sleeping with Chicks*

*Don't Sleep with Your Drummer*

# YOU
### are a
# BADASS
### at
# MAKING
# MONEY

## MASTER THE MINDSET OF WEALTH

# JEN SINCERO

**life**

PENGUIN BOOKS
An imprint of Penguin Random House LLC
375 Hudson Street
New York, New York 10014
penguin.com

First published in the United States of America by Viking Penguin,
an imprint of Penguin Random House LLC, 2017
Published in Penguin Books 2018

ISBN 9780735223134 (paperback)

THE LIBRARY OF CONGRESS HAS CATALOGED THE
HARDCOVER EDITION AS FOLLOWS:
Names: Sincero, Jen, 1965- author.
Title: You Are a Badass at Making Money : Master the
Mindset of Wealth / Jen Sincero.
Description: New York : Viking, 2017. |
Identifiers: LCCN 2017009015 (print) | LCCN 2017021065 (ebook) |
ISBN 9780735223004 (ebook) | ISBN 9780735222977 (hardback) |
ISBN 9780735224209 (export)
Subjects: LCSH: Finance, Personal. | Self-actualization (Psychology) |
Self-help techniques. | BISAC: SELF-HELP / Motivational & Inspirational. |
SELF-HELP / Personal Growth / General. | BUSINESS &
ECONOMICS / Personal Finance / Money Management.
Classification: LCC HG179 (ebook) | LCC HG179 .S486 2017 (print) |
DDC 332.024/01—dc23
LC record available at https://lccn.loc.gov/2017009015

Printed in the United States of America
13  15  17  19  20  18  16  14  12

Set in Bembo MT

For Gina DeVee, whose wise guidance, loyal friendship, and relentless ass-kicking helped me out of the garage and into a whole new financial reality.

# CONTENTS

# CONTENTS

# YOU
### are a
# BADASS
### at
# MAKING
# MONEY

# INTRODUCTION

I f you're ready to make more money, you can. I don't care how many times you've tried and failed or if you're so broke you're selling your bodily fluids for bus fare or how often you've found yourself center stage at the checkout counter, feigning shock and indignation: "Are you sure? *Declined?!* That's impossible. Can you run it one more time?" No matter how out of the question it may seem for you at this moment, you can make lots of money. Even I'ma-buy-everyone-I-love-a-house-and-a-gold-tooth kind of money, if that's what turns you on.

I'd also like to point out that there's nothing horribly wrong with you if you haven't figured out how to do it yet. Money is one of the most loaded topics out there—we love money, hate money, obsess over money, ignore money, resent money, hoard money, crave money, bad-mouth money; money is rife with so much desire and shame and weirdness it's a wonder we can utter the word above a whisper, let alone go out and joyfully rake it in. (Have you been brave enough to read this book in public, I wonder? With the title in full view?)

It reminds me a lot of how we've been conditioned to deal with sex, another gold medalist in the Topics That Totally Freak People Out Competition. When it comes to having sex and making money, you're supposed to know what you're doing and be all great at it, but nobody teaches you anything about it, and you're never supposed to talk about it because it's inappropriate, dirty, not so classy. Both money and sex can provide unthinkable pleasures, birth new life, and inspire violence and divorce. We're ashamed if we don't have it, we're even more ashamed to admit we want it, we will do things/people we're not nuts about in order to get it, and I know I'm not the only one who has caught myself fantasizing about a stranger dressed like Batman coming up and giving me some on a bench in Central Park (am I?).

The good news is if you, like most people, have a troubled or conflicted relationship with money, you have the ability to heal it, transform it, and become such awesome pals with money that you wake up one day to find yourself standing in the middle of the life you've always wanted to live. And you can start making this change right now. All you need to do is wake up to what's holding you back, make new, powerful choices about what you focus on, ensmarten yourself about money, and go for it like you ain't never gone for it before. Which is what this book will help you do.

I personally transformed my financial reality so quickly

and massively that everybody who knows me well is still wondering what the hell happened. And believe me when I say if my broke ass can do it, you can do it too, no matter how rickety or hopeless you may feel right now. Because I knew precisely zero things about making money until I was in my forties. My forties! That's the age when most people possess things like houses and college funds for their kids and an understanding of how the Dow Jones works. Meanwhile, at forty I possessed a barren bank account, a deep wrinkle line between my eyebrows from stress, and a first-name basis relationship with Sheila at the collection agency.

For the vast majority of my adult life I was a freelance writer, forever scrambling for work that paid an insulting nonamount considering how time consuming and challenging it was. Had I actually done the math, I would have realized just how free my lancing was, but I instead chose to be in denial of the facts, work harder, complain more, and just, you know, hope that I'd somehow magically start raking in the dough or get run over by someone rich who would then have to take care of me for the rest of my life. My watertight plan for getting out of financial struggle was partly based on having a whole lotta hang-ups about money (money is evil, rich people are gross, I have no idea how to make it, I'd have no idea what to do with it even if I did know how to make it, etc.), as well as my perpetual, and torturous, state of indecision. I knew I was a writer, and I also knew I wanted to do more than sit alone in a room in my robe and type all day, I just didn't know what it was I wanted to do. And rather than just picking something already and seeing where it led, I chose to bite my nails down to bloody nubs and wallow in the I Don't Know What the Hell I Want to Do with My Life quagmire. For years. As in decades. It was so painful. And devastating. And utterly paralyzing. This is how I found myself at the ripe old age of forty, living in a converted garage, in an alley, in fear of requiring dental work, excelling at financial mediocrity in the following ways:

- Eating/drinking/filling my pockets with anything that was free, regardless of whether or not I really liked it or needed it.

- Walking countless blocks, in flip-flops, to save five dollars on valet parking.

- Employing duct tape, instead of professionals, to repair things like leaking pipes, busted shoe straps, and fractured bones.

- Meeting friends at a restaurant for dinner, ordering a glass of water, tap is fine thanks, I love the tap in this city, before explaining to the table how I'm really not hungry, I'm stuffed actually, and then the free bread is placed on the table and disappears into my mouth in a blur.

- Choosing between phone service and health insurance.

- Spending excruciating amounts of time purchasing anything, from a TV to a bedspread to a wooden spoon, in order to thoroughly investigate every possibility of a cheaper option, a forthcoming sale, a coupon code, or to entertain the question, "Is this something I could perhaps make myself?"

If I'd put the same amount of time and focus that I put into freaking out about not having money, cutting back my expenses, finding the deals, haggling, researching, returning, refunding, redeeming, rerouting, rebating, into actually making money, I would have been driving a car with working windshield wipers years before I actually did.

This making money thing is not about never again making wise, informed purchases or rejoicing in a good sale or filling up on bread. It's about giving yourself the options and the permission to be, do, and have whatever lights you up, instead of acting like a victim of your circumstances. It's about not pretending everything is cool, I love having three roommates, none of whom know how to use a sponge or a goddamned broom, instead of focusing on making more money to afford yourself your own place for fear you'll be judged or you'll suck at it or that it'll be too hard or no fun or out of your reach. It's about creating the wealth that affords you the life you'd love to live instead of settling for what you think you can get.

The human ability to rationalize, defend, and accept our self-imposed drama is bananas. Especially because we have all the power within us to choose and create realities that totally kick ass. We see it all the time with people who are in miserable or even abusive relationships: "He's just so sad and sorry after he cheats on me. It breaks my heart. Plus, the make-up sex is superhot." We see it when people insist on staying in jobs they hate: "I spend my lunch breaks weeping in the stairwell I'm so miserable. But the health insurance is amazing." Meanwhile their spirit and their time on this Earth are quickly swirling down the drain.

······································································

Time wasted rationalizing the mediocre could be
time spent creating the magnificent.

······································································

You have one glorious and brief shot at being the you that is you on Planet Earth, and the power to create whatever reality you desire. Why not be the biggest, happiest, most generous, and fully realized humanoid you can be?

After some forty-plus years of scraping by, I finally could no longer bear hearing myself say my mantras of choice, "I can't afford it" and "I don't know what I want to do," or to continue living in places so crappy and small that I could sit on the toilet, answer the door, and fry an egg all at the same time. (It was like living on a boat. Or in a toadstool.) I could no longer sit back and watch all these other people out there kicking butt, making great money doing what they loved, treating their pals to fancy dinners, donating more than five bucks and a thank-you note to charities they loved, traveling the world in luxury, wearing shoes that no stranger had worn before—basically living the life I wanted to live. I was just as smart, talented, charming, well groomed . . . What the hell was my problem? What was I *waiting* for? No matter how much I complained or freaked out or tried to convince myself that my present rickety life was as good as it could, should, or would get, deep down I knew I was meant for, and wanted, bigger things. I'd get all excited hearing about someone's cool job as a globe-trotting journalist or hanging out at someone's beachfront house and think, *This! This could be me!* And instead of using that excitement to propel myself into action, I immediately started talking myself out of going for it. *Well, I have nothing well written enough to show that I could be a good journalist. And I'm not entirely sure that's what I want to do. Plus, I have a cat. I could never travel the world and leave Mister Biggins behind.* Even though staying stuck where I was felt easier and less risky than putting myself out there, it also felt awful. I felt like I was letting myself down, being a wimp, holding back, denying myself a whole lot of awesomeness, snoring my way through life. Because, basically, I was.

The knowledge that I could be doing so much better, but wasn't, finally became so unbearable that I got off my butt and made the hell-bent-for-glory decision to get over my fear and loathing of money and figure out how to make some. And to let myself do it in a way that maybe wasn't perfect, but that at least felt sort of right, instead of clinging to the easy out of being unsure. There was no thunderclap "aha" moment; I didn't narrowly escape dying in a grease fire or get dumped by the love of my life for being such a loser or have some big "snap out of it!" epiphany. I just suddenly couldn't take listening to myself complain anymore. I just finally woke up. Which is how the desire to make massive change kicks in for most people.

The leaps I had to take to catapult myself out of my safe little reality were often terrifying and hugely confronting. For example, I invested alarming amounts of money in putting an online business together: taking courses, hiring mentors, building a Web site, getting headshots taken by someone other than my right arm, etc. I risked looking like an idiot and a fraud because this new business of mine was all about coaching other writers and I'd never coached other writers before. I risked losing the aforementioned alarming amounts of money on building an online business because I knew not one thing about running online businesses. Or off-line businesses for that matter. Even telling people that I had a damn business felt ridiculous. It felt pretend, like I was just playing office until someone busted me: *Just kidding! Sorry! I don't really know what I'm doing!*

But no matter how scary each step was, it was nowhere near as frustrating as constantly wondering how I was ever going to pay off my student loans or feeling like I was wasting away in my tiny little life when I knew I could be doing so much better. I'm now not only making seven figures as a success coach and author, but I'm writing a book on how to make money. Me, Jen Sincero, ex-shoplifter and scrounger for coins in couch cushions (other people's couch cushions)—it's as unthinkable as my ninety-year-old father becoming an overnight sensation on *Dancing with the Stars*. And then writing a book about it. Miracles. I believe in 'em.

One of the coolest things I remember is how quickly, once I made the no-nonsense decision to get my financial poop in a scoop, new opportunities and ideas and income streams started showing up in my life. They were there the entire time, of course, I was just too busy clipping coupons and focusing on my ennui to notice. But I want you to know that you have everything you need right now to start turning your financial reality into something that doesn't make you wake up screaming in the middle of the night. You just have to be willing to do what it takes. And here's what it takes: Agreeing to get really really really really uncomfortable. Over and over again.

We've been raised to believe that you have to work hard to make money, and certainly there are times when this is true, but the real secret is you have to take huge, uncomfy risks. You have to do stuff you've never done before, to make yourself visible, to acknowledge your own awesomeness, to risk looking stupid. You must not only admit to desiring, and commit to creating, wealth, but, most important, you must allow yourself to do so. Taking risks is uncomfortable, but it's the kind of discomfort that's equal parts *eeek!* and *hell yeah!* Fear and excitement are two sides of the same coin, and that is precisely the kind of discomfort I'm talking about. Otherwise known as a rush, it's the critical, thrilling discomfort of living large and in charge.

My hope for you is that you read this book over and over and do everything it says, that you listen to the hollerings of your heart instead of your doubts and fears, and that you continuously leap bravely into the unknown. I've seen countless clients and friends and people I meet at parties in such struggle around money, it's like watching people starve to death when there's an all-you-can-eat buffet just down the hall. The money you desire is here for you. The opportunities, the clients, the teachers, the brilliant moneymaking ideas, they're all right here, right now, waiting for you to wake up, let them in, and get this party started.

# CHAPTER 1

# ALLOWANCE

I have a friend who has an extensive owl collection. It all started when she innocently purchased a wooden carving of an owl in front of her mother one afternoon. "Hmmm, isn't that cute?" Her mother, in turn, sounded the family rallying cry, the news spread like wildfire, and my friend is now the horrified owner of owl potholders, owl clocks, owl earrings, owl slippers, *I don't give a hoot!* T-shirts, needlepointed owl pillows, owl salt and pepper shakers, stuffed owls, owl soap-on-a-rope . . . on birthdays, holidays, and graduations, the dreaded flock descends, perching on her shelves, flapping up her wall space, peeking out from her closet—it's like a horror movie.

"I don't know how it got so out of control," she moaned one day as she unwrapped an *Owl Always Call You Friend* cross-stitch wall hanging from her sister-in-law. This went on for years before she finally got up the nerve to put a stop to it, to thank them very much, but declare her world an owl-free zone from now on. Her friends and family were surprised, hurt, and indignant, and although the onslaught eventually stopped, they treated her like she was nuts. "Fine, if that's what you want, but . . ."

People love to tell you what you should and shouldn't want, regardless of how you feel about it. Even worse, we're so malleable, if we listen to them long enough we'll tell *ourselves* what we should and shouldn't want, regardless of how we feel deep down. If we're not careful, we can stay stuck for years, or even lifetimes, in situations that cause us pain because we'd rather defend these nontruths than upset or disappoint anybody, our own inner critics included. We'd rather do what's expected of us than give ourselves permission to be, do, and have what feels good and right and awesome.

For example, when I made one of my first attempts at crawling out of my lifelong financial stink-hole, I ended up crawling right back in even though I so desperately wanted out. My attempt involved a book entitled *The Science of Getting Rich* by an old-timey guy named Wallace Wattles. I don't remember what inspired me to finally pick it up, it could have been anything—when my cat needed stitches I couldn't pay for and I was too grossed out to sew him up myself? When I lost my ability to turn my head to the left and decided it was time to start sleeping on a mattress instead of my futon from college? That time I accidentally regifted a pair of candlesticks to the same person who'd given them to me and I vowed to only buy people presents from that moment forward? What I do remember, word for word, is the very first sentence of this book. Because as I sat reading in my living room/kitchen/dining room/bedroom/guest room, the first sentence of this book leapt out and spat in my eye, offending me to my core. It said this: *Whatever may be said in praise of poverty, the fact remains that it is not possible to live a really complete or successful life unless one is rich.* Whatever! Wattles! Plenty of people are poor and happy and feel complete and successful!

The fact that I myself was poor, and that I felt far from successful or complete as a result, was apparently beside the point. The point was I'd spent an entire lifetime self-righteously insisting that being rich was overrated and gross, and I wasn't going to back down easily no matter how broke I had to stay in order to prove my point. I could handle the idea of making more money, but saying that one had to be rich? That was unacceptable. I was so disgusted that Wattles could be such a shallow ignoramus that I not only slammed the book shut and didn't pick it up again until years later (at which time it, erm, totally changed my life), I also continued to barely make any money for those next few years.

Instead I kept toiling away, taking the odd low-paying job here and there, writing articles, catering, babysitting, knitting, attempting to sell what I knitted, etc. As torturous and time consuming and totally *ain't getting rich anytime soon* as my plan was (example: cost of yarn + time it takes to knit a kaftan + charging anything less than five thousand dollars for said kaftan = seriously not worth it), it was still apparently more worth it to me to keep doing things the way I was doing them than it was to work on my negative beliefs about money and change what I was doing. I was more attached to my truths about how evil money was, and to my beliefs about my ability—and my right—to make money, than I was to my desire to no longer shop for groceries at the dollar store.

In my seasoned experience as a grouchy broke person, and my many years of coaching countless people on the topic of wealth, I've discovered that few things make people want to fight, vomit, or ask for their money back more than telling them that one must be rich to be successful and complete.

.........................................................................

One of the biggest obstacles to making lots of money is not a lack of good ideas or opportunities or time, or that we're too slovenly or stupid, it's that we refuse to give ourselves permission to become rich.

.........................................................................

I see it over and over, the kicking and screaming about how, at the end of the day, what's most important is spending time with those you love, gazing at sunsets, rejoicing in the laughter of frolicking children, helping old ladies cross the street, and other things money can't buy, and I won't argue, but I will ask this: Why the hell does this come up when we discuss the making of money? When did it become an either/or situation? If you partake in the pursuit of wealth, it's not like you shall never again attend a family barbecue, hug a puppy, or tiptoe through the tulips. In fact, if you do it correctly, you'll be able to afford to spend even *more* time on such merriments. And do it in style! Not to mention pay for the gas to put in your car to get to the family barbecue, buy the hot dogs, show up wearing clothes, and marvel at Uncle Carl's famous card tricks unfettered by thoughts of your crushing debt or how you're going to hit him up for a loan to cover your rent this month as soon as he's had a few beers.

Everybody arrives on this planet with unique desires, gifts, and talents, and as you journey through life, your job is to discover what yours are, to nurture them and to bloom into the most authentic, gleeful, and badassiest version of yourself. In order to do this, as a human being in modern society on Planet Earth, you must be rich. And let me clarify what I mean by rich lest you think I'm saying your life is worthless unless it involves a mansion and a yacht:

RICH: Able to afford all the things and experiences required to fully experience your most authentic life.

While the amount of money you need will depend on who you are and what you desire, ain't nobody riding for free. No. Body. We exist in a world where, like it or not, nearly everything involved in your growth, pursuit of happiness, and self-expression costs money. If you're an artist, for example, your riches might go toward things like paint, canvases, brushes, a studio, trips to places that inspire you and fill you up with ideas, dinner out with friends and fellow artists to keep your spirits and energy high, hiring a PR firm, someone to walk your dog so you can work, a personal trainer, and a DJ at your art opening, paying the admission fees to museums, buying healthy food, music to listen to, classes, glasses, and a beret.

What you need is a very squirrelly subject, heaped high with guilt and confusion and fears, and the only person who can answer what you truly need to be the most joyfully you is you. The trick is getting clear amidst the endless supply of inner, and outer, opinions. For example, maybe you've had an experience similar to this: You've just hung out at someone's lavish home and left feeling like, *I want my house wired for sound with speakers in every room too! How have I been living this long without it?* Only to visit with a friend soon thereafter who's wearing the same clothes she wore in college more than twenty years ago, who's driving the same falling-apart car and listening to the same crappy stereo, because she feels these things are good enough, why create more waste by throwing them away and upgrading? And you suddenly find yourself feeling dirty for wanting a big fancy stereo and speakers in your laundry room.

There will never be a lack of conflicting opinions and information when it comes to any decision you make in life, and this is especially true when it comes to something as controversial as money. Depending on who we were raised by, the society we grew up in, and the people we surround ourselves with, our minds can be littered with thoughts that have us believing everything from the critical importance of making big bucks to keep up with the Joneses to existing on crumbs and sleeping on a camping mattress in order to be a noble, good person. All that matters is what's true for you, which is why getting really good at listening to your intuition and your heart, and following your happiness, is critical. And which is why I want to drive home the following point: If you allow yourself to make all the money you need to flourish and live out your desires, it does not mean you are, or will become, a greedy, selfish, Earth-ruining bastard.

..............................................................

A healthy desire for wealth is not greed, it's a desire
for life.

..............................................................

Desire literally means *de sire*, "of the father," and whether or
not you believe in God, your desires were bestowed upon you
when you became your earthly self, along with other distinc-
tive you-type things like your face and your personality and
your affinity for needlecrafts. They are unique to you, they
define the essence of who you are, and they act as the road map
for your life. Your desires were given to you by the Universal
Intelligence that created everything in existence with the express purpose of being carried out by you during your lifetime.

As a member of the human species, you are part of nature,
and everything else in nature is provided with all it needs to
carry out its desire to thrive and flourish, so why wouldn't
you be? Nature is a fine-tuned, well-thought-out machine
that is all about the fullest expression and perpetuation of life.
Mother Nature gets an A+ in systems management and resource replenishment, she's got it down; it's when mankind
gets freaky and scared and greedy that nature is thrown out
of balance. We pollute, strip, and destroy our dear pal the
Earth in horrifying and often irreparable ways when we act
from fear instead of the desire to collaborate with our planet
and the creatures on it. We hoard resources because we fear
there aren't enough to go around or that we're unworthy unless we have more more more. We pollute our water, air, and
land and ravage our forests in order to cut costs or make lots

of money because we're unconscious, insecure, and hence, power obsessed. While it's impossible to live on Earth and not make some sort of impact, if we humans were all in harmony with our highest selves, feeding our desires instead of our fears, in the flow with Mother Nature, giving and receiving in a healthy, collaborative, conscious way, this planet would be in beautiful shape.

All of nature is forever moving, growing, changing, reproducing, evolving—it's all the rage, even the damn Universe itself is expanding. Likewise, you are not meant to just survive, to stay stagnant, to settle; you are meant to keep growing and thrive. Just like the tree that sucks up nutrients, water, and sun, grows to its tallest, mightiest height, and drops shit all over our yards that will then spawn the next generation of trees, and the frog that miraculously grows from egg to tadpole to adult, you too are meant to reach your fullest expression of the you that is you, to inspire and birth awesomeness in others, and to use whatever resources you need along the way.

........................................................

**We all have seeds of unthinkable badassery inside of us, yet only some of us will allow ourselves to grow.**

........................................................

The difference being, of course, that, unlike the tree and the frog, you are human. So unless your truth involves living in a cave on rent-free land, carving images of caribou on the wall with a pebble while dining on nuts and berries not owned by Monsanto, pretending that you can reach great heights without the proper funds is cray. In fact: If you are here to become the grandest, most generous version of yourself, which you are, and if that costs money, which it does, it is your *duty*, as a hallowed child of Mother Nature, to get rich.

Even if we could live on what's within reach, sitting under an apple tree next to an endless stream of fresh water full of fish with a cocktail waitress stopping by every couple of hours, eventually we'd get bored, seek new lands, want to go for a bike ride or something. Humans are curious by nature, our desire to keep evolving physically, mentally, and spiritually is part of who we are, which is why settling, staying stuck in a rut, treading the lukewarm water of mediocrity (or worse) is so excruciating.

...................................................

All of Mother Nature's creatures are designed to fully flourish before they drop dead.

...................................................

You, just like all living things, are meant to take up space on this planet. Shrinking back and denying yourself the things that bring you great joy, living under a cloud of guilt, refusing to make an impact ain't why you're here. The Earth is not here for us to pillage, but it is here for us to enjoy, care for, and appreciate. You living your fullest life and making all the money required to do so doesn't take anything away from anyone else any more than you refusing a ham sandwich because someone, somewhere, is starving, helps them.

........................................................

Greed comes from the same lack mindset as poverty.

........................................................

Staying broke because you fear it's gross to be rich or that you don't deserve money or that you getting rich somehow prohibits someone else from getting rich too is all rooted in lack. Lack is the state of being you're in when you believe you're in need of, when you believe that what you desire doesn't exist, when your outlook on life is a *glass with a hole in the bottom* as opposed to a *glass half full*. A lack mindset believes that there's not enough to go around, that you're not good enough or worthy enough to flourish, that the money you spend may never make its way back to you, etc. Pigging out on money and things and experiences is also based in fear and lack—fear of never having enough, fear of not being secure, fear of being unlovable, trying to fill a bottomless hole in your heart. Nothing in excess is healthy: Gluttony is just as devastating as is anorexia. You denying yourself your heart's desires is not noble, it's a waste of some damn good desires. And it denies the world our only opportunity to bask in more of you.

If you sometimes feel hopeless because of all the pain and suffering in the world, and worry "Who the hell am I to get rich when others are starving and being bombed out of their countries and enslaved?" know this: One of the best things you can do is get rich. Because of the way our world is structured, money and power are intertwined, so if you want to help make a positive change, money is one of the most effective tools you can use to do it. Yes, you can donate your time, organize, protest, lobby, alert the masses, post incensed rants on Facebook, but you will be much more effective if you have the energy, options, and freedom that come with not being in financial struggle, not to mention the resources to spend however you see fit. Instead of complaining and freaking out about the power-mongering, greed-obsessed fatheads who are perpetrating such harm on the planet, and handing them even more power by staying broke because you don't want to be like them, why not focus yourself on getting rich instead so you can make a big difference? You can do some really cool stuff with money; don't let the jerks who give it a bad name ruin it for you.

You cannot give what you do not have, so if you want to help others you have to take care of yourself first. This is why they always tell you on airplanes that you have to put your oxygen mask on first before you help someone else with theirs. They have to remind us of this because it's counterintuitive—unless you are a sociopath, it's your *nature* to help. Few things light up the human heart like helping/ bringing joy to others. Trust in the fact that when you're well taken care of financially, you'll be even more poised, and inspired, to spread the love.

Our world, now more than ever, needs as many compassionate, creative, bighearted, conscious people to be as rich as possible so we can turn this mother around. I mean, imagine if you and all the people you love and respect had assloads of money? And if they felt grateful and empowered by it, not icky and guilty? And if they could afford to spend it on themselves and others and on saving our planet in ways that uplifted everyone involved? Please take a moment to really envision the specifics of this as it pertains to yourself and the spectacular people in your life. Take them all one by one and imagine how they'd feel, who they'd become, what they'd spend their newfound wealth on. If yer peeps are anything like mine, it makes the whole concept of being rich something worth writing a love song about.

........................................................................

There is no such thing as too much awesome.

........................................................................

I'ma go ahead and say it out loud (join me, won't you?): I love money. There's no need for explanations or apologies. I also love pizza and I can say that without tacking on a bunch of disclaimers: *I love pizza, but, you know, it's not everything. Spending time with people you love and being of service are important too.* Let's take back the word "money" and decriminalize it, because until you do, you aren't going to be terribly motivated to let yourself make much. I've been broke and sad, rich and sad, broke and happy, rich and happy, and I'll take the rich version over the broke version all day long. Because money gives you freedom and options and I really love freedom and options. Who doesn't?

While we're at it, let's go ahead and decriminalize rich people, shall we? Contrary to popular belief, the rich are just people, they're not intrinsically filthy, nor do they deserve to be killed, eaten, or robbed. We live in a society that's made a sport out of judging people with lots of money, so regardless of how you feel in your conscious mind about the rich, i.e., *Some of my best friends are rich!* it's important to be aware of any negative beliefs you may be harboring deep down. Of course, there are some rich people who totally suck, but some of them are awesome, just as some poor people totally suck and some of them are awesome. The problem is that it's socially acceptable to roll our eyes when someone drives by in a Bentley or talks about how very many dollars they made this year, meanwhile it's part of normal conversation to complain about how broke you are or to announce that you got your boots for a mere five bucks at Goodwill. Snobbery works in both directions—if you're rich, thinking you're better than those who aren't is as equally lame as being broke and thinking you're better than those who are rich. Start paying attention to any disparaging comments that may fly out of your mouth, or your mind, when it comes to rich folk, because if you plan on becoming one of them it's gonna be a whole lot easier if you actually approve of who you're becoming.

Take a deep breath, trust your desires, and embrace the fact that your quest for riches is a quest to become more of who you truly are. We don't all desire to live a huge, fancy life or solve world hunger, that's not what this is about. It's about you letting yourself be the biggest badass you can be, whatever that happens to look like for you. You are meant to thrive, and by thriving you automatically help others to thrive too. Think about it: Just standing next to someone who's being totally who they are, who is lit up by life, who goes for it fully, who believes anything is possible, who is excited to be in on the adventure of spinning around on this planet, who allows themselves to look stupid, to fail, to succeed, to be rich, to be generous, to basically be, do, and have all the things and experiences that make them the most themselves—it makes you feel like you could go out and flip over a car, right? So why not be that for someone else by being the most you that you can be too?

If you're a political activist, be as active as you can possibly be, if you're a musician, rock on with your bad self, if you're an attorney, fight for what's right, if you're a stay-at-home mom, raise awesome kids with great manners. It all counts, it all contributes, we're all equally vital, it's not a competition. There wouldn't be room for all of us to do all of the same things the same way, which is why we each desire to fill our own special spot in the world with our own special selves. Understand that your gifts, talents, and desires were given to you because you are meant to thrive and share your youness with the world as only you can. Please oh please, allow yourself to get as rich as you need to be in order to bestow upon us your greatness.

### SUCCESS STORY: IF HE CAN DO IT, SO CAN YOU.

*Charles, 54, went from making $20,000 a year to over $145,000 a year in less than seven months:*

I always thought I loved money, but I realized after a while I had a problem with it because I never made any. After some serious introspection I realized that because I grew up poor in a broken home and my father never paid us a cent in child support, the message that I received, and came to accept as truth, is that I'm not worth anything. So throughout my life, as opportunities came along I would somehow allow that underlying belief to sabotage any success.

I started saying mantras of encouragement to myself about my greatness, and would express thanks to the Universe, to everybody and everything around me, for things that I hadn't received yet. And it changed me, it elevated me to be a more positive person, and I went forward doing things that I didn't believe were possible, but I did them anyway. I also began learning skills to improve myself, some at a great expense.

I practiced interviewing for jobs by doing hundreds of interviews until I got good at it. One thing that helped is I looked at the others around me, even the ones hiring me, and found that I was a great deal more knowledgeable and better skilled than even they were. My confidence slowly began to develop.

I continued interviewing and landed my present job, where I make over $145,000 a year.

Today, I'm living in the best home that I've ever lived in, my children are all in the best schools that they have ever been in, I drive the best car that I have ever owned, and have luxuries that I had never imagined would be possible. My doubts about my self-worth still rise up every now and then, but I keep working on it and know I can beat it. It's an amazing feeling.

## TO GET RICH

Suggested Money Mantra (say it, write it, feel it, own it):
*I love money because I love myself.*
Please give at least ten answers to each of the following:

1. Make a list of all the reasons why you deserve money.

2. Make a list of some beautiful things that have happened in this world thanks to money.

3. Make a list of all the awesome things and experiences money will add to your life.

4. Make a list of how you being rich will benefit others.


Please fill in the blank:
I'm grateful to money because _____.

# CHAPTER 2

# WHY YOU AIN'T ROLLIN' IN THE CHEDDAH. YET.

When I was a kid, every so often my parents would get my brothers and sister and me all dressed up, file us onto a plane, and off we'd go to visit my dad's side of the family in his hometown of Naples, Italy. I have such vivid and random memories of those trips—my first-ever glass of blood-red orange juice, unthinkably purple and delicious, that I sipped on the balcony of our hotel room with my bare feet up on the railing. My grandfather's giant green parrot, who screamed at us in Italian (In Italian! A bird!). My Aunt Lucia, greeting us with her arms lifted high over her head in prehug enthusiasm and the shocking mound of armpit hair thus revealed, the likes of which I'd never seen on a lady and which was so terrifyingly obscene to my American sensibilities it was as if she'd greeted us by spreading her legs in my face.

During one of these trips, when I was around seven years

old, my Uncle Renato took the whole gang out to his favorite seafood restaurant, someplace overlooking the water with a big patio full of picnic tables. The horde of Sincero cousins, siblings, aunts, uncles, in-laws, and grandparents vied for prime placement around two long tables, and by some stroke of luck, amidst the chaos, I managed to score the most coveted seat of seats, right next to my dad.

My father was the focal point of everything on these trips, not only because he was like a celebrity: the dashing eldest son returned home with his beautiful American wife, proud brood, and successful doctor's practice, but mostly because he was the only one who spoke both Italian and English. Which meant that every time anyone said anything, four long rows of picnic benches and twenty sets of eyes were transfixed on him, blinking in eager hopes of him translating some witticism or anecdote that would allow us to turn to one another and laugh, nod, and feel that sense of tribe that families who actually understand what the hell one another is saying feel.

Right after we were seated, the owner or chef or someone important came up to our table and made a big show of greeting Uncle Renato, who was clearly a celebrity in his own right, and there was much handshaking and cheek pinching and *benvenuto*-ing before the man clapped his hands together, announced, "Welcome, my frens! I hope you are hangry!" and disappeared inside the restaurant. Moments later, a steady stream of food that would continue nonstop for the next four hours began appearing in front of us.

At some point the waitress brought over a plate that was

piled high with deep-fried circular somethings, and my dad pulled me onto his lap and told me to try one.

"What is it?" I asked.

"Just try it."

"Yeah, but what is it?" Instead of telling me, he turned to the rest of the table, pointed at the plate, and rattled off something in Italian, the only parts of which I understood were the words "Jennifer," "*mangia*," and the laughter that ensued. Now there were four rows of picnic benches and twenty sets of eyes staring at me and this stupid plate of fried circles that I was suddenly terrified of. My father, in spite of his celebrity status, is a pretty shy guy, and truth or dare isn't really his scene, all of which made me think that whatever was on that plate must be really bad if he was willing to put on this big a to-do about it.

My mind immediately went to worms. It couldn't possibly be anything else. You hear all the time about these foreign countries where they eat things like tarantulas and eyes and brains, so, of course, some people must eat worms. I imagined how one could easily make a circle out of a worm, dip it in batter, and deep-fry it. I mean, what other creature could you do that with? The answer: Only worms.

As deeply disturbing as this thought was, I hated being teased, and I hated losing at truth or dare even more, so in front of the entire Sincero Nation, I popped a mystery circle into my mouth and chewed, gagging and wincing while waiting for the worm to explode. But much to my surprise, there were no guts, instead it was more like eating a rubber band—chewy and tasteless and dumb. My father then yelled in my face, "It's squid!" and everyone erupted in laughter and applause and my Aunt Alberta patted me on the head and I retreated into a deep, seething blackness of hatred and humiliation that had me up and bolting for the bathroom in a fit of tears.

I was a kid who liked fish. Had I known the truth about what I was putting into my mouth I could have avoided the gagging, the drama, and the scolding I got later that evening for kicking my brother hard in the shin when he imitated me trying to choke down a worm. Which brings me to the point of this story:

........................................................

Our "realities" are make-believe—whatever we make ourselves believe, we experience.

........................................................

When it comes to forming, and transforming, our human experience, the power of the mind reigns supreme over any type of external "truths." If you believe money is evil and/or difficult to make, your bank account will have tumbleweeds blowing through it. Strong religious beliefs inspire everything from wars to glorious houses of worship to cutthroat charity pie-baking contests. The belief that you are hot and sexy will have you getting hit on by strangers on the street. And if you believe you're eating worms, you will gag.

There's a neuroscientist named Vilayanur Ramachandran who uses the power of belief to help amputees in excruciating pain find relief. Many people who've lost a limb experience what's called phantom pain—very real pain sensations in a part of their body that no longer exists. Because the limb is no longer there, there's no way for them to massage it or soak it or do anything to relieve the pain—hello how freaking torturous is that?

Through the use of mirrors, Ramachandran reflects the image of a patient's existing limb to where the missing limb used to be, so it appears that the missing limb is no longer missing. Then, if they're missing an arm, for example, they move their existing arm, unclench their hand, relieve the tension however they can, and the mind is tricked into believing that this is happening to the missing arm and the pain disappears. By making the mind believe that the nonexistent exists, he is able to help his patients change their physical reality.

......................................................
**Your external world is a mirror of your internal world.**
......................................................

If you can make yourself believe the thoughts that are screwing up your financial life, i.e., *I can't make money because of X (I'm a single mom, I live in the middle of nowhere, I'm an idiot, etc.)*, you can make yourself unbelieve them too. This is how powerful we are and how deceptively simple changing our lives is—we can literally create the reality we desire by making ourselves think and believe what we desire to think and believe. How awesome is that?!

Our beliefs, along with our thoughts and words, are at the root of everything we experience in life, which is why consciously choosing what rolls around in your mind and falls out of your mouth is one of the most important things you can do. This conscious choosing of your thoughts, beliefs, and words is called *mastering your mindset*, and master it you must if you'd like to live large and in charge instead of being bossed around by your circumstances.

Here's the lowdown on how your mindset works.

## BELIEFS

When it comes to money, most people feel like their beliefs are in pretty good shape: *Hell yes, I will gladly let you give me money all day long, thank you very much—here, I just so happen to have a bag for you to put it in!* But what they don't realize is that this is their conscious mind talking, and that deep down we all have our subconscious mind, which is the motherboard that controls all of our results. And if mama ain't happy, ain't nobody happy, so no matter how much you may think you're all about the money in your conscious mind, if your subconscious believes that you will get cut off from all family gatherings if you get rich because as a kid that's what you saw your jealous grandfather do to your dad when he got rich, you ain't gonna be rollin' in it anytime soon. Here's why:

### THE LITTLE PRINCE

The subconscious mind is like a seven-year-old prince who suddenly becomes king when his father dies: He's running the kingdom of your adult life based on information that he gathered, and processed, while doing somersaults and pulling down his pants in the front yard. Meaning, he didn't really process any of it at all.

When you're born, you don't have any attitudes and beliefs about money. You arrive blank, open, game for anything. You base your "truth" about money on what you learn from the people around you and the experiences you have. All this information flows into your subconscious mind before your brain has matured and developed any sort of filter or analytical ability to be like, *Hold on a minute, just because Mom and Dad fight about money all the time doesn't mean money is bad. It could mean he's jealous that she makes more than he does. Or that she wants him to pay more attention to her so she picks fights with him.*

When you're a kid, all this information comes in through a much simpler, kid-sized perspective, meaning you take what's right in front of you at face value. So, with this example where you grew up seeing your parents fight about money, you might believe money = fighting = scary = bad. Or: *If I make money, I will be yelled at and unlovable.* Or: *Money scares the hell out of me because it looks like someone's about to get hit every time the topic comes up.* And this information, in this very basic, emotional form, gets lodged in your subconscious mind like a meat cleaver as the truth. And there it remains for the rest of your life (unless you reprogram it, which I will show you how to do later), serving you well if it's positive and helpful, and frustrating the crap out of you if it holds you back from creating the life you desire.

Here are the three basic attributes of the subconscious:

**It's primal.**

The subconscious mind's number one concern is survival. As a little baby who can't take care of or fend for itself, losing love and being abandoned literally equals death, so anytime we come near to putting ourselves at risk, the Little Prince goes crazy and tries to stop us. This is one of the main reasons we stay stuck in lives we're not nuts about—we don't wanna risk trying and failing, trying and succeeding, losing weight, getting rich, having a new opinion, a new love life, a new strut in our step for fear the people we love will reject us when we change. While this may work for a little kid who's doing the best he can to survive, it sucks for an adult.

**It's sneaky.**

Most people have no idea that they've got all these underlying beliefs holding them back. They're only aware (somewhat) of their conscious thoughts, so they work on those and leave the real culprit beneath undisturbed. This is how we get trapped in our patterns—dating the same weirdos over and over, repeatedly working for people who treat us like poo, spending all our money the second we make it: The Little Prince, and your unquestioned conscious beliefs, are ruling the roost.

**It doesn't want to be dethroned.**

And your Little Prince will pitch a full-on temper tantrum if it looks like things are headed that way. Let's say you make the bold decision to quit your job as a kindergarten teacher and open the day-care business of your dreams. You put very clear and no-nonsense financial goals firmly in place, set about securing a loan to rent a space, come up with a name, like, perhaps "Who Cares? Day Care," and neatly get all your ducks in a row. Meanwhile, beneath the surface, if you believe that struggling is more noble than succeeding because that's what your parents taught you, and that everyone who loves you as you used to be will judge and abandon you when you're rich, your subconscious self might attempt to "protect" you by suddenly getting the flu, by picking fights with people who can help you, by inspiring you to procrastinate, make terrible investments, drink your face off the night before (or morning of) an important meeting, etc.

When you change who you're being, you're basically killing off your old identity, which completely freaks your subconscious self out. Change hurls you into the unknown and puts you at risk for all sorts of loss and, of course, all sorts of unthinkable awesomeness, which is why it brings your biggest fears to the surface.

Your Little Prince is desperately trying to keep you in a safe, known space, otherwise known as your comfort zone, but if the truths you're running your life on no longer fit who you're becoming, it's like trying to squeeze into the snow pants you wore as a kid when you're thirty-six years old. Not so comfy after all. Yet we do it all the time because even though they cut off our circulation and hold us back from who we so desperately want to become, the puffy pants are familiar, cozy, and feel safer than trying on an outfit that we've never worn before. We are so attached to the unhelpful familiar, in fact, that we will spend our valuable, very finite time here on Earth crafting excuses to keep ourselves right where we are, instead of leaping into the glorious unknown and growing into who we're really meant to be.

..............................................................................

**The walls of your comfort zone are lovingly decorated with your lifelong collection of favorite excuses.**

..............................................................................

Love your Little Prince for being a great pal by trying to protect you, but it's time to step into your power, put on your grown-up crown, and take your kingdom back.

Along with our overbearing Little Prince, the quest for Earthly security holds people back from living the lives of their dreams more than almost anything else, and the ridiculous part is *it doesn't even exist*! People will spend lifetimes slogging it out in "secure" jobs they hate, staying in relationships with people they don't like rather than risk being alone, never spending money on anything fun in order to save it for a rainy day, meanwhile we are flying through outer space in an infinite Universe on a planet prone to earthquakes and plagues and ice ages. That secure job at that secure company could dry up, some lunatic could run up and start beating you to death with a tree branch—anything could happen at any time.

Now, of course, focusing on this wouldn't be helpful in living a productive or happy life because we'd be crouched under tables and clinging to buildings while trying to walk down the street, but I'm reminding you of it in hopes of liberating you from the pointless, oftentimes life-sucking trap of sacrificing living your dreams for false security. To free your heart up to follow your joy and ride the wave of awesomeness instead of limiting yourself and playing it safe.

> Trying to protect yourself from your fears protects you from experiencing a fully evolved and juicy life.

I'm not talking about putting yourself in harm's way, pooh-poohing safety precautions, or acting like an irresponsible maniac—*Screw it, we're all going down anyway, let's cash in the kids' college funds, buy a bunch of blow, and drive to Mexico!* I'm talking about freeing yourself up to thrive in abundance instead of living life clinging to your fears. I'm talking about focusing on your heart's desires, on infinite possibility, on enjoying the crap out of your life instead of worrying about what you might lose.

Be responsible, put money aside for the future, wear your seat belt, make big, fun plans with your friends and family, don't walk through shady neighborhoods alone, invest your money wisely, exercise your body and your mind, practice safe sex, don't smoke cigarettes or get drunk in public and bad-mouth your neighbors—act as if you've got a long, happy life on Earth ahead of you. But do not shrink back from something you desire because it's too risky. Just being alive is risky.

Allow yourself to experience whatever your heart desires as if this is your one and only chance to take the ride of your life.

## WORDS

Our perception of reality is also greatly influenced by our words. Words bring our thoughts and beliefs to life and help anchor them into our "realities" through repetition. Words help us form our identities; we get attached to our lingo, our schtick: *My memory is crap. I left the keys in my front door again— what a choob!* The more you tell yourself you're a forgetful choob, the more you will believe it, and hence, act like a forgetful choob. You tell a kid that she's stupid enough times and she'll believe she is, even if she just taught herself to read in Chinese. I told myself pretty much every day for forty years that I had no idea what I wanted to do with my life and, as a result, remained in the fetal position of hopelessness and confusion for decades. Had I replaced the phrase "I don't know" with "Clues are all around me!" I would have opened myself up to receive tidbits of clarity instead of slamming the door on lawd only knows how many golden opportunities.

....................................................................

What comes out of your mouth comes in to your life.

....................................................................

Because we are creatures of habit who tend to have our words on repeat, they become like a chisel that forms grooves in our minds, playing the same stories over and over, anchoring in our thoughts and beliefs and defining our reality. Our words are like water flowing over rocks—over time they have the power to create grooves the size of the Grand Canyon. This is what I love about the phrase *stuck in a rut*—you're literally stuck in a rut or a groove of thought, beliefs, and words, and in order to free yourself, you need to consciously create a new groove, and a great place to start is by getting yourself some new, better words.

Language defines and shapes our perception of reality by giving it an understandable structure. We create, and reinforce, boundaries around time, for example, talking about what we did yesterday, how tomorrow can't come fast enough, and how *someday I'm gonna start eating healthy but right now I'm going to explore what a cheeseburger tastes like with a slab of butter on it,* etc. Meanwhile, according to Einstein, time is an illusion, it's flexible, nonlinear, and the whole twenty-four hours in a day thing is a giant hoax. We've all heard this before yet we are a staunch seven days in a week, fifty-two weeks in a year kind of culture, and this is made "real" by our language. The Hopi people, who perceive the world more in tune with Einstein's findings, have no words in their language to express the past or future because they basically exist in the now. In fact, they don't even have a word for "now" because to step back and call it something would take them out of the moment. There are countless realms of reality, and the words we use wrap us up nice and tightly into whichever perception we're participating in.

Words also have an incredibly persuasive effect on us. Think about how incredible it is when someone speaks directly to what you're feeling or thinking or fearing. The right words spoken at the right time can make you feel recognized on a deep soul level, and can be so powerful as to inspire entire nations of smart people to vote idiots into office or a whole community to drink lethal Kool-Aid. So start paying attention and notice if you're repeatedly announcing how much you hate/fear/mistrust money via language such as: *I'm an idiot when it comes to money, I could never afford that, I hate that rich bastard,* etc. If you're bad-mouthing money, you're gonna want to go ahead and knock that off.

## THOUGHTS

Your thoughts inspire emotions that inspire action
that forms your "reality."

When I was little we lived next door to a family with a bunch of kids close to my age. Their parents were German, and while I was playing at their house one day a couple weeks before Christmas, they let me in on some very valuable information. Apparently, not only were there presents to be had under the tree on the twenty-fifth of December, but there was another holiday they celebrated in Germany at the beginning of the month, called Saint Nicholas' Day, and if you left your shoe outside overnight, it would be full of presents the next morning. Hello!

I immediately went home and picked out the biggest shoe I had, a clog, waited nine million years for the rest of the day to go by and dinner to finally be over so I could sneak outside and leave my clog right next to the front door as instructed. As I lay in bed that night listening to my parents clean the kitchen, my heart suddenly leapt out of my chest at the sound of the front door opening and the dog being called. In a matter of moments my name was being called too.

"Jennifer! Get your butt down here right now!" My mother was standing at the bottom of the steps waving my clog over her head, demanding to know how it ended up outside. I mumbled something about taking it off and forgetting to bring it in, apologized, and slinked back upstairs with my freezing-cold shoe. Great. Now I'd have to sneak out again after they went to bed and risk getting in twice as much trouble. Yet as serious an offense as it was—it was a brand-new clog on top of everything else—and as grave as the repercussions would no doubt be, it was totally worth the risk. Because . . . presents. The story ends with me getting no presents, obv, getting busted again thanks to the stupid dog, who needed to be let out early to pee, and being put on a full month of hamster-cage cleaning duty as well as dishwasher-emptying duty, made all the worse by the glee it brought my newly chore-free siblings.

We are creatures who are driven by emotion. When we're all fired up, we ain't listening to nothing else, not wisdom and logic or fear and doubt. Our emotions compel us to participate in staggering displays of both the magnificent and the moronic: We will flip over parked cars in the street when our team wins the World Cup, date people covered in red flags, spend hundreds of dollars on a beautiful pair of shoes that don't fit, risk a second round of scolding from our parents for leaving our clogs outside, etc. We will also accept an exciting new job that we're "unqualified" for, overcome our fear of flying to visit a friend in need, step onto a stage in front of hundreds even though we're terrified, go into the red to launch the business of our dreams, etc. You cannot have an emotion without having a thought first (e.g., *We won! I love my friend! I wanna be my own boss!*). When you learn to master your mindset and focus on thoughts that elicit strong, positive emotions, you wield your power to take crazy leaps of faith in spite of your fears and your Little Prince trying to hold you back. It all starts with your thoughts; they are the catalyst that brings on the shift that changes what you believe and how you act.

To get a better idea of what I'm talking about, here's a breakdown of how your mindset works:

Your beliefs are driving the bus. They take you where you're going whether you're paying attention or not.

Your thoughts are the tour guide, the person up front with the microphone and the clipboard—she can lean over and yank the wheel, slam on the brakes, step on the gas, flip the bus—she can do whatever, whenever she wants. She usually works in harmony with your beliefs, but she has all the veto power.

Your words are the assistant to your thoughts and beliefs. Your words back them up, voice their opinions, anchor in their message, keep it real.

Your emotions are the fuel. They are ignited by your

thoughts, and can change your beliefs and the direction of your life. Without emotions, yer going nowhere new and exciting.

Your actions build the road. They pave the path for your beliefs, but will reroute should thoughts and emotions make a change of plans and decide they want to stop at Dairy Queen or something.

When all these facets of your mind, body, and spirit are in alignment, focused on the same desire, singing "Ninety-nine Bottles of Beer on the Wall" as they merrily roll along, you can manifest all the riches you desire. But if you're thinking about how much you'd love to make an extra five thousand dollars a month and how you have no idea how to do it, if you're feeling terrified and extremely doubtful, believing that people won't take you seriously (yourself included), if you're saying out loud "I love money and it comes to me easily" every morning in the mirror, and if you're making one sales call per day after which you give up and crack open a beer, you ain't gonna get very far.

All members of team mindset must be on the field bringing their A game, yet it's your thoughts, and I hate to play favorites here, that are the biggest badasses of them all.

In order to get your thoughts working at their max potential, let's take a look at some of the most common beliefs about money that we often unconsciously accept as the truth and blab away about all the livelong day. Pay attention to which of these remind you of something you may have heard yourself thinking or saying, because awareness is the first key step in breaking the spell of your not-so-awesome financial "reality."

Here's the drill:

- Become aware of what your limiting thoughts and beliefs are.

- Question and investigate them.

- Rewrite them.

- Say it out loud and proud.

I'm going to do this for the first few so you can see how it works:

Unhelpful thought: *Money can't buy happiness.*

Question: *What makes me happy?*

Answer: *Hanging out with the people I love, grilled cheese sandwiches, being loved and loving others, laughing my ass off, giving great gifts, traveling, hiking, playing with my dog, taking road trips, listening to music, drinking beer, having my own business, leaving huge tips, freedom, getting massages.*

Question: *Does having money help me achieve any of these happy things?*

Answer: *Yes.*

Rewritten thought: *Money supports my happiness.*

Unhelpful thought: *I'd rather focus on having fun than making money.*

Question: *Is it fun when you make money?*

Answer: *Yes, when I make it it's fun, but what I have to do to make it isn't fun.*

Question: *Would it be worth your time, during your one and only life, to find or create an occupation that is fun?*

Answer: *Yes.*

Question: *Do you understand that anything you set your mind to is possible, even having a job that is lucrative and fun?*

Answer: *Yes.*

Rewritten thought: *I make making money fun.*

Even if you're not 100 percent on board with believing these new stories yet, do you feel how much more emotionally uplifting they are than their original sad sack versions? Do you understand how shifting the narrative with the same diligence a mechanic might replace a busted carburetor isn't a bunch of pain-in-the-ass busywork, but something that can help you make real transformation in your life?

Here are some other commonly held beliefs that are real winners, and that may sound familiar to you. Pick whichever ones sound like something you'd think or say and reframe them:

You can't be rich and spiritual.

Money isn't important, people are.

Never go into debt.

Save your money for a rainy day.

Rich people are lucky, gross, selfish, entitled, snobby,
    shallow, egomaniacs, holier than thou.

You have to work hard to make money.

You can't make money doing X (whatever you love to do).

I'm too irresponsible, lazy, clueless to make money.

It's not polite to talk about money.

It's important to have a good, secure job.

If you get excited by making money it means
    you're shallow.

Money doesn't grow on trees.

You must go to a good college to make money.

Money causes stress.

There's never enough money.

Money is trouble.

I don't want to be a sellout.

You have to sacrifice having a good/fun life to
    make money.

Money is out of my reach.

You have champagne tastes on a beer pocketbook.

Always have a backup plan.

It's lonely at the top.

Who has that kind of money?

He/she is only about the money.

Imagine walking around experiencing similarly icky thoughts and feelings for something just as omnipresent as money. For example, what if you thought these things about the sky? *The sky is the root of all evil, it's not polite to talk about the sky, loving the sky makes me a bad person, the sky turns otherwise decent people into pigs.* You'd barely be able to leave your house, let alone relish the joys of life.

When you (consciously or unconsciously) resent money or cling to your limiting beliefs about money or refuse to participate in making money, it does not serve you, it does not make you more noble, it does not help you or anyone else. What it does is put you on a hunger strike by cutting you off from that which you need not only to survive, but to thrive. By embracing money and getting into the flow, you open yourself up to the abundance that is trying to reach you this very moment.

---

**SUCCESS STORY: IF SHE CAN DO IT, SO CAN YOU.**

*Here's a great story from Sandra, 44, who put more faith in what she desired to believe than what she was raised to believe:*

I used to live in my truck in the Midwest. I now live in my dream beach house in California and am a successful actress.

My main limiting belief around money was that if I made lots of it, my life would get too complicated and I wouldn't know how to handle it. You know, math, taxes, investments, etc. I was afraid that money, beyond necessity for the day, week, or month, would be

---

more than I could understand or control. I didn't feel smart enough or good enough. Blah-blah yawn.

Step One: I got up and did the work. Thoughts and beliefs are key. I got clear about my fears around money and hammered myself with new beliefs like: I love and approve of myself, I am open to all the good and abundance of the Universe, I know what I'm doing, I deserve success and respect and awards and money and the best the world has to offer, there is plenty of money and prolific prosperity for everyone—especially me. . . .

Step Two: I aligned with mentors and hired people who knew how to handle the stuff I didn't know about, was scared of, or disinterested in. I focused on being me, creating and delivering something of value to the world. I let other people handle the selling of it, the business of it, the legal of it, but kept my eyes open so I didn't get screwed out of what was mine.

Step Three: I fell down and got back up more times than I ever imagined. I am still falling down and learning how to get back up. Success is not an end-of-the-road game. It's a never-ending-road game. I am practicing seeing and feeling the success fully—as if it's already done, won, and in the bank.

Love yourself because you are the only one of you ever. Do something badass with the you you have got. Even if people think you're crazy. Whatever it is you decide to do, do it with joy, gumption, and dedication so it will be your moneymaker and your merrymaker.

## TO GET RICH

Suggested Money Mantra (say it, write it, feel it, own it):
   *I love money and money loves me.*

1. List the five main things you remember your parents telling you about money.

2. Take any negative thoughts that came up for you in the first step above and break them down (as I showed you how to do earlier in this chapter on page 44).

3. Rewrite your new truths about money.

4. Take the new truth that has the most charge for you and write it down every morning and every night, feel it in your bones, repeat it in your head as often as possible, say it out loud, keep hammering yourself with it until it sinks in.

5. Notice how you've been clinging to security in a way that's holding you back in any part of your life. This could be dating someone who you know isn't the right person, never letting yourself spend your money on something fun, doing anything that bores you to tears because you want to be liked/you feel you "should"/you'll be judged if you don't, being scared to tell your blabbermouth neighbor that stopping by unannounced is unacceptable, etc. Find something that's not serving you that you've been scared to let go of because of the security it provides, and take the first step in letting it go. This is large, Marge, so if

you can't think of anything off the top of your head, stick with it until you do. It could make a gigantic shift in all areas of your life.

Please fill in the blank:
I'm grateful to money because _____.

CHAPTER 2A

# A TINY BUT MIGHTY CHAPTER ABOUT UNIVERSAL INTELLIGENCE

There is no lack of opinions and theories when it comes to the Universal Intelligence that created, and continues to create, all that exists. Some people call this mighty power God, some call it Spirit, some call it a load of crap. If you're one of those people who happens to be skeptical about buying into such woo-hooery, and you desire to get rich, I strongly suggest you put your grouchiness aside and agree to take some new beliefs for a spin. Because not only could you very possibly see gigantic results by partying down with Universal Intelligence, but I'm telling you, whether you like it or not, you already sort of believe in it. You believe in something, somewhere. Whether it's fate or luck or divine intervention, you've knocked on wood before. You've said a prayer when your team's about to lose or you suddenly notice blue and red flashing lights in your rearview mirror. You've thanked someone named God before or stuck an *oh my* before his name while watching a video of an old lady jump over a pile of her grandkids on a skateboard. You've gotten a magically knowing hint from somewhere. "I don't know what made me think to stop off at Mom's house on the way home, but if I hadn't she'd still be lying on the floor." You've caught a glimpse that there might be something out there that you can't totally wrap your head around, that is participating in our lives with us. You've felt it tickle the hairs along the back of your neck. Even if it's just the tiniest smidgen of recognition, you've said howdy to Universal Intelligence.

The reason I'm insisting on this is because once you acknowledge that there's a force larger than your physical self at play in your life, you can start working with the highfalutin and limitless power of the Universe to make some money around here. We've been taught to treat the information delivered to us via our five physical senses as the truth. Meanwhile, without sounding like an ingrate for all the awesomeness provided by my eyes, ears, nose, skin, and tongue—seriously, guys, huge thanks—these senses of ours are limited. Our senses provide only a certain scope of information limited by the reach of those senses. For example, our sense of smell is far inferior to a dog's. A dog can smell a package of salami being opened the second the seal is broken. From the other room. While sleeping. Bats can totally make fun of us right in front of our faces at frequencies too high for us to hear. Cats and their bionic night vision will always beat us in an after-dark obstacle-course competition. Most people define their reality from the confines of what their five senses tell them, but there is so much more going on, like, say, an infinite, eternal Universe worth of stuff.

Just like electricity and gravity—two things that impact our everyday lives that we don't actually see, that few of us understand, and that, hello, everyone believes in anyway—Universal Intelligence and the power of our thoughts are real and affecting our lives every single moment. You show your faith in gravity by not flinging yourself off roofs and your faith in electricity by not picking at a light socket with a fork. You may not understand the intricacies of how it all works, but still, you're totally down with following the rules. I want to encourage you to follow suit with the information I'm giving you now—put it into practice as you embark on becoming rich and let the results speak for themselves. Because trust me, once you start experiencing how powerful your thoughts and Universal Intelligence are, even though you may not totally grasp the entire WTF of everything involved, you'll be down with the program when you're rollin' in the dough.

We live in a Universe that is made up of energy, everything is vibrating, moving, changing, and buzzing. This goes for all that's visible as well as all that's unseen: this book, microwaves, your car, a brick, thoughts, money, words, a rock, a peck of pickled peppers, etc. One of the ways we interpret this energy is via our five senses: Our eyes pick up on light energy, our ears translate sound waves, our touch interprets energy as solid mass, etc. But this is only an interpretation of reality, and a limited one at that. This interpretation of our reality is also run through the filter of the belief system we've formed via all the information we've picked up over the course of our lives. Between our five physical senses and the "truth blueprint" created by our belief system, our perception of reality is, shall we say, a tad limited.

Here's the thing that makes me so excited to be alive on planet Earth as a human being with a conscious mind: We have the power to participate in the realm of reality that goes far beyond what our truth blueprint tells us, what our five senses tell us, or even what a dog's, cat's, or bat's senses tell them. And the way we blast beyond this limited realm is with our thoughts.

Nothing happens or comes to be without being thought first: our staggering solar system, your favorite song, the amount of money in your bank account, all of it. Our thoughts are linked to the invisible energy that makes up all that is, and they help mold it into that which we experience on the physical plane. And here's the real humdinger: Universal Intelligence and your thoughts are basically the same force—just as the water droplet that lands in the ocean is part of the whole sea, so your thoughts exist as part of Universal Intelligence. In other words, you are one powerful motherfucker.

...................................................................

The invisible world creates the visible world.

...................................................................

The more conscious you are about thinking powerful thoughts, and the less you're caught up in the limited aspects of the illusion created by your five senses and your truth blueprint, the more in-tune and connected you are to Universal Intelligence, and the more ease you will have in getting rich. The way you communicate with and stay connected to Universal Intelligence amidst the distractions and mayhem of your daily doings is through two types of thought: outgoing thought and incoming thought.

## OUTGOING THOUGHT

We are the only creatures on Earth with the power of conscious thought, and we use it to mold our realities and our paychecks by alerting Universal Intelligence that *this is how it is*. Universal Intelligence created all that is and all that will be, and your thoughts are how you use your free will to harness the power of Universal Intelligence to mold your reality. If you send out thoughts like, *I can't afford to go on vacation and I don't see that changing anytime soon*, the Universe is like, *Noted! You can't afford it. Stuck at home it is!* Just as your thoughts created the financial reality you're experiencing right now, you can also use them to overpower what "is" to manifest whatever reality you set your mind to. And I mean whatever you set your mind to. This is because everything you can think of already exists in the Universe, otherwise you wouldn't be able to think it. I know, bananas, but stay with me here.

All information, physical, mental, and spiritual, originates from the same source: Universal Intelligence. Where are your thoughts before they come into your mind? Where is the flower that grows out of the teeny tiny seed? Where is the reality of you doubling your income with your awesome new cat costume business? All of this already exists in the energetic realm, and it's through our minds—and how our mindset inspires us to take action—that the new reality is made to manifest on the physical plane. If you can think a thought, that thought already exists. And since all things come from Universal Intelligence, that thought must exist in a physical form as well. If you have a desire to make fifty thousand dollars, that money, and the way for you to make it, already exists. Otherwise you wouldn't be able to think it up in the first place because the thought of the money, and the money itself, are the same stuff. This concept is a 3,897-page book with a prayer mat and a bucket of ayahuasca thrown in, but for the sake of our work here, this is the gist of how Universal Intelligence works.

Your thoughts dictate the truth. So if you're presently living in your mother's basement working at the Chicken Shack down the road for $7.95 an hour, and you fixate your thoughts with unwavering determination on owning your own two-hundred-acre chicken farm and a Cadillac, that chicken farm and sweet ride are your truth. Your thoughts alert Universal Intelligence to start arranging the energy in such a way as to make your desires manifest in physical form (you need to learn how to see and receive the new opportunities that will lead you to your goal, which we will go into more deeply later). Your thoughts also trigger your emotions, which get you off yer ass to take action, and your reality begins to shift. This is how people in wheelchairs climb mountains and those who grow up in extreme poverty become rich—they consider their thoughts to be the truth, regardless of how their "reality" may appear, get all worked up into an excited tizzy about it, and make it happen. They use the power that all of us have to create what they desire instead of settling for what they see surrounding them.

..................................................................

Opportunity is in the eye of the beholder.

..................................................................

Mastering the mindset of wealth is choosing to think about money, and your reality in relation to money, in a way that will make you rich, not keep you poor.

When you consciously focus your thoughts on the wealth you desire, imagine yourself rolling around on a big ole leaf pile of Benjamins, feel how right and good and exciting it feels to be in the financial flow, you arrange the energy around you, and within you, to vibrate at a high frequency, and, as a result, your reality mirrors back to you high frequency opportunities and things. You can feel this energy, it literally lifts your spirits and pulls into your radar all the high frequency opportunities and things you shut yourself off from when you're all low vibe and sad sacky about your wimpy bank account, your lack of job options, your botched attempt at trying to get a raise, etc. Meanwhile, thinking about how amazing it's going to feel paying off your fifteen-thousand-dollar credit card debt, telling yourself *I'm so grateful this card is paid off in full I can hardly stand it* over and over, writing out an actual check for the precise amount to pay it off and looking at it every day, all of these thoughts arrange the energy around you to vibrate at a higher frequency and to take the physical form of that which you're focused on: fifteen thousand dollars. These positive thoughts release your resistance to having the money come in—you're on board, you're believing it, you're feelin' it, you're lovin' it! Once resistance is gone, you're back into your natural state of flow, there's no doubt and fear cluttering up your energy, and the Universe can deliver you the riches you desire.

## INCOMING THOUGHT

The Universe is constantly showing up, cup of coffee in hand, wanting to discuss how to increase your finances and offer a helping hand. It connects with you:

Via your intuition: *I just know in my gut that I should buy this house even though it costs way more than what I wanted to spend. It still feels right.*

Via synchronicity: *I wonder what ever happened to Janet from cooking class. Oh look, there she is, calling me right now.*

Via inspiration: *Check out this awesome idea for a song that just popped into my head out of nowhere!*

Via desire: *I just know I'm meant to be rich even though none of my screenplays have sold yet.*

Via coincidence: *I just opened a book to the perfect page—it's exactly what I needed to read!*

If you are truly committed to kicking ass, you'll want to strengthen your relationship with the Universe in the following ways:

- Learn to quiet your mind and receive the information it's trying to send you.

- Trust that this information (aka your intuition) provides all the answers you're seeking no matter how terrifying/bananas/unacceptable they may seem.

- Surrender and have faith that when you bravely head into the unknown, the Universe has your back.

- Accept that you don't have to know how to do what you don't know how to do yet, and that the Universe will lead the way.

..............................................................

We all have the ability, through our thoughts, to harness the power of the Universe.

..............................................................

If that doesn't have you heading out to purchase a superhero cape and tights, I don't know what else I can say.

## CHAPTER 3

# SHOW ME THE MONEY

Early one morning while visiting my mother, I came downstairs to find her standing in the kitchen in her bathrobe, empty coffee cup in her hand, frown on her face.

"We're out of milk for coffee," she informed me flatly, clearly unamused by the prospect of getting dressed and cleaned up for the brief walk down the hill into town. She announced that she'd rather just head to the store wearing her damn robe, sneakers, a baseball cap, and too much orange lipstick, and finally commit to becoming, as she put it, an interesting town character. "I'm in my seventies, I think it's time."

Mom has one of the most delightful senses of humor I've ever experienced, and is hilarious in general, which is why I was so surprised when she phoned one day to inform me, mortified, that she'd just learned what the word "twat" meant. Really? I thought. Hadn't she been calling my brother one for years? But she was upset for real, utterly devastated, unable to find one funny thing about a word that is—come on—funny.

This call came in during a time when my mother was an active member on the board of trustees in her historic and charming suburban town. During her tenure, she pleaded her case on issues that were near and dear to her heart, such as protecting her favorite park from falling into the hands of developers, planting daffodils in the median on Main Street, and keeping the road signs along the scenic town reservoir to a minimum.

Apparently it was preserving the integrity of the reservoir that caused her to place this particular call of distress to me, while facedown on her bed, mumbling "Oh God" over and over through her pillow into the phone. From what I could make out, earlier that day she'd posed an argument to a roomful of upstanding and respectable fellow trustees that went something along the lines of this: "It's a slight bend in the road, why do we need five, FIVE, signs with arrows on them before, during, and after the curve to alert people to the fact that they need to turn slightly to the left? The signs are an eyesore and a waste of taxpayer money and if you're that much of a twat that you can't navigate the road without an arrow every two feet, you shouldn't be driving." I was then to learn that this was not the first time she'd paraded the word "twat" before the esteemed council—she had apparently been flinging it around for years in response to the twats in the mayor's office responsible for passing her least favorite ordinances, the high school twats who spray-painted *Class of 2003* on the sidewalk in front of the deli, and, most passionately, the stupid idiot twat of a drunk driver who took out a phone pole on Elm Road last Halloween.

"I thought it meant 'twit,'" came her muffled voice. "And Ginny Adams, the head of the garden club and a full-fledged twat in the truest sense of the word, thank you very much, is the one who pulled me aside and told me to clean up my act. Oh God." By taking a stand to end the twittery in her community, my poor mother not only discovered the power of choosing her words wisely, but she discovered that she'd unwittingly become an interesting town character.

When you don't investigate what's going on with your words, thoughts, and beliefs, you risk stumbling through life on autopilot. You may, for example, automatically assume that your beliefs are founded in your own truths rather than perhaps the truths of your parents and/or the people around you. Or that your words accurately express your beliefs, instead of being mindless regurgitations of stuff you've heard before or proof that you have a lousy handle on vocabulary. And don't even get me started on how much time we waste spinning out on thoughts that are, shall we say, less than productive. Once you wake up, become aware of your thoughts, beliefs, and words, and start choosing them wisely, you can avoid staying stuck in a life of excruciating ho-hummery (or worse), constantly being in financial struggle or, as in Mom's case, getting reprimanded for having a potty mouth by someone who is a far inferior gardener than you are.

....................................................................

When we don't master our minds, we risk building
our lives on a foundation of flimsiness.

....................................................................

Mastering your mindset is important in all areas of your life, and it's especially critical when it comes to money because money plays such a massive role here on Earth. We literally can't function without it. Realizing you've left the house without your wallet is as alarming as realizing you've left your journal on the subway or forgotten Grandma at the truck stop. Not a day goes by where we don't use money, or use something that was paid for with money, or have an experience that is somehow connected to money. Not. One. Single. Day. Money's in the roads we drive on, the food we eat, the music we listen to, the freedom we enjoy, the adventures we have, the babies we birth, the showers we take, the poems we write, the noses we blow—it's everywhere, like dust or temptation or hormones in high schoolers.

And yet we rarely, if ever, stop to investigate how we feel about money, how we speak about it, or even what the hell money actually *is*.

So I'ma stop right now.

## MONEY IS A MEDIUM OF EXCHANGE

Back in ancient times, before the invention of money, people exchanged goods and services by bartering. They'd do things like build a stone wall for someone in exchange for a pile of animal pelts and a bag of salt or trade you a castle for a couple of your daughters. Then it basically got to be too much of a pain in the ass to carry around pelts and rocks and took too much time to build stuff so the humans came up with the idea of money, assigned a value to the coins and notes, and now all you have to do is reach for your wallet instead of five of your best camels if you want to buy a car or something.

Money is a unit of measurement used in the act of giving and receiving. Contrary to popular belief, money itself is neither good nor bad, friend nor foe, filthy nor clean—it's just blank, minding its own business, trying not to get jammed in a soda machine. Money is just the messenger. It's what you do with it and how you think, feel, and speak about it that give it a personality. And depending on the personality you give it, you're either gonna want to surround yourself with it or stay the hell away from it.

Which is why thinking money is bad or dirty (without, erm, really thinking about it), and reinforcing these thoughts by speaking badly about it, is one of the leading causes of serious brokeness. For example, here's a little sumthin' you may have thought and/or said before:

Money is the root of all evil.

Yes, our world is full of unspeakable horrors and injustices born out of the things people do for money, but the wrong-doing is caused by the perpetrators, not the money. It's like deciding cars are intrinsically evil because people turn into obscenity-hurling jackasses behind the wheel or that vegetable peelers are hateful just because you sliced your finger open with one once. Money, cars, and vegetable peelers are also conduits for great joy, tasty adventures, and they all make excellent wedding gifts.

In the words of the late, great Ayn Rand: *Money is only a tool. It will take you wherever you wish, but it will not replace you as the driver.*

There are lots of words in the English language whose meanings sort of seep into each other. It's easy to get confused about where one ends and the other begins. For example: love/lust, being nice/lying, confident/drunk. When it comes to the desire to make money, the most common term people confuse it with is "greed," especially when discussing the root of all evil and other such unpleasantries. With all of these examples, taking a moment to discover the truth can save a lot of disappointment and heartache. So let's be clear:

Greed: *An insatiable, excessive, selfish craving for more more more.* Another term that's oft confused with money is "power mongering": *Wielding influence in a tyrannical and supermean way.* And let us not forget ye olde "corrupt": *Morally bankrupt, focused on personal gain whilst giving nary a crap how your actions affect others or what the law says.*

Here are some other popular ways people use the term "money" incorrectly:

Money ruins everything.

Money and friendship are like oil and water.

Money makes monsters out of otherwise good people.

Pretty harsh, right? It's not like money broke into your house and punched you in the face fer fek's sake, it's just trying to help you buy stuff. Here's something else that's important to realize about money if you're going to go out and make a whole lot of it.

## MONEY IS CURRENCY AND CURRENCY IS ENERGY

Money is a blank slate that gets its value from the energy and meaning we give it. For example, the fifty bucks you make by raking leaves for the lady across the street has a very different energy than the fifty bucks you steal out of some guy's pocket on the subway. The same ratty chair you'd buy in a thrift store for five dollars might be worth five thousand dollars if David Bowie had had it on his tour bus. Some artists charge two hundred dollars for their paintings, other artists charge twenty thousand. When you get hired to do something and realize halfway through that you way undercharged, your payment, when it finally comes, feels like you're being handed a soggy napkin. Or if you way overcharged, it makes you cringe, feel lowdown and dirty. And if you charge the perfect amount, you feel uplifted, like a supastah. Giving and receiving money is an energetic exchange between people, and your job is to consciously get your frequency in alignment with the money you desire to manifest and open yourself up to receiving it. This means getting clear on the value of the product or service you're offering, being excited and grateful instead of weird and apologetic about receiving money for it, and having total faith that this money is on its way to you instead of worrying about the possibility of its not showing up.

Here's an important concept to understand: Money always comes to you through other people, but it comes from Universal Intelligence, as do all things. Which is why focusing on the frequency of your thoughts, not the people you hope to make money from, is the key to getting rich. For example, let's say you need to make four thousand dollars to fly Grandma first class to the quilting convention in Nova Scotia that she's always dreamed of attending. You've decided to sell your unopened Obi-Wan Kenobi figurine to raise the money, and you've got someone seriously interested in buying it. Raise your frequency to match the frequency of the four thousand dollars coming toward you instead of focusing on the particular person you hope to get it from. Focus on the fact that you're giving someone the most awesome piece of *Star Wars* memorabilia, complete with double-telescoping lightsaber, in exchange for the money you desire and deserve. Imagine Grandma chatting up the folks in first class, sipping her free champagne, soliciting suggestions on which fabric swatches to use for her quilt. Your focus needs to be on your desire for this money and what it's for, your excitement to share something of value with someone in order to obtain the money, your clarity on how joyful it will make that person, your gratitude that this money is coming to you, oh hell yes it is, and your belief that the Universe has got your back.

..........................................................

People are to money what a French fry is to ketchup:
They're just the conduits.

..........................................................

Not only is it none of your business to try to make anyone do anything, but focusing on a particular person who may or may not be the conduit for the money you seek potentially cuts you off from the person with the big bag of money that the Universe is trying to connect you to. It's like deciding that you're going to attract the love of your life. You focus on the qualities this person has, your excitement over being with him, your glee that he too is searching for you, you do things like smile more often, doodle little hearts on everything, leave the house smelling like a wedding bouquet—this is your job description. You do not spend your time trying to convince the uninterested hot guy from the coffee shop with the motorcycle and nothing in common with you that you are his one true love, thereby missing out on the awesome guy at work with the big nose who's perfect for you in the process. Same goes for making money—you do the energetic work, get your thoughts, actions, and words in line with what you desire to create, and surrender the rest of the details up to the Universe.

It's all about the energy of exchange. I learned so much about this back in the day when I'd give my pals the friend discount/freebie for my coaching services. Devaluing my work gave them an easy excuse to devalue their efforts: They had no incentive to rise to the occasion and really push themselves because they literally weren't invested. I ended up doing all of us a disservice by lowering the frequency around the money instead of demanding we all put on our big people pants and pony up. These "favors" were a big fat waste of time for everyone involved and could have been avoided if I hadn't come from a place of feeling weird and shamey about charging my friends.

Because money is currency and currency is energy, when you shrink down and lower your prices to accommodate someone, you're basically saying the equivalent of "I don't think you could grow and manifest the money you desire to work with me. I don't believe you're that powerful. I also don't think I have the right to charge what I'm worth or to make the decisions around here about what to charge." Not discounting my rates doesn't mean I don't donate my money and services, offer scholarships, put things on sale, etc., but I only do it if the energy around it is clean, aka coming from a place of power and possibility instead of insecurity, shame, can't, lack, I'm a greedy, bad friend, etc.

Money is a renewable resource. It comes and goes, it ebbs and flows, it's meant to move. When we're cheap about spending it or weird about receiving it, we block its natural course, we put ourselves in a place of lack instead of abundance, our energy becomes richus interruptus. Even something as minor as leaving a big tip for a waitress, or picking up, instead of passing by, a quarter laying on the street, or letting your neighbor pay you for watching her dog all day, which you totally would have done for free—that's all coming from an energy of abundance and a healthy, happy appreciation for money. What you focus on you create more of, so if the plan is to get rich, you're gonna want to focus on abundance as much as possible. Give as much as you can as often as you can, receive with gratitude and joy, think of money as your pal, raise your frequency and get in the flow, yo.

---

**SUCCESS STORY: IF HE CAN DO IT, SO CAN YOU.**

*How Joe, 40, attracted money to himself and went from making $40,000 a year to over $100,000 a year:*

When it came to increasing my income, I was my biggest block. I didn't think I deserved money and was overly critical of myself, which resulted in self-destruction.

I started reading and listening to lots and lots of self-help books. My morning commute was an hour at the time and I would listen to at least two hours daily. My turnaround started when I realized how much the Universe/God wanted to give me all I wanted. Then I had to get out of my own way, because the trick is that you have to really want it too, to the point where you believe that it's already yours.

I work in a corporate setting and I started moving up the chain once I applied myself and shifted my mindset. I took on more responsibility and got out of my comfort zone as much as possible.

What keeps me going is remembering why I started doing the work that I do in the first place—because I

---

love helping people, I love using my brain, I love being challenged on a regular basis, I love the camaraderie at my office. I also remember that I don't want to be stuck in the same place as I was when the project started. The sense of accomplishment is like a drug.

Before, money was difficult to get, now money is all around me and I attract it. I normally pay for everything via credit card, however I make it a point to have some cash in different places in my house at all times. Not so I can necessarily spend it, but more to set an unconscious reminder that money is everywhere and all I need to do is reach out and grab it. I know . . . corny, right . . . but for me it works. It helps take away the anxiety when unexpected things happen and things get tight. Get over the fear—get to the root of the fear and deal with it.

## TO GET RICH

Suggested Money Mantra (say it, write it, feel it, own it):
*I love money because it's the root of so much awesome.*

1. Write down five positive words to describe money.

2. Practice saying thank-you every time you receive money, think to yourself, "See, money loves me, it just can't stay away," do a victory lap around your house, kiss your checks, celebrate the momentous gift of being in the flow with

abundance—what you appreciate appreciates. Do this whether money is sent to you in the mail, shows up as interest on an investment, is handed to you by a person, etc. Relish the feeling of gratitude and the joy of being in the flow with money.

3. Spend at least five minutes every day sitting in silence connecting with the energy of money. Imagine money flowing all around you, filling you up, moving into and out of your heart. Also, walk around all day feeling into this as much as possible.

4. Leave money around your house in various places so you get used to seeing it all the time. Remind yourself how abundant it is. Make it like an Easter egg hunt.

Please fill in the blank:
I'm grateful to money because _____.

# CHAPTER 4

# BEST PRACTICES FOR
# BUSTING YOURSELF

Somewhere along my journey through overcoming my financial flimsiness, I attended a weekend seminar called Manifesting Money Like a Millionaire! I don't remember the specifics, but it was probably in Las Vegas, probably in some fairly cheesy hotel conference room, definitely outside my comfort zone. There was about a three-year period in my early forties when I went to these types of things all the time. This particular event happened sometime after I started my online business helping writers get their book proposals done, before my business broke six figures for the first time, and months after moving out of chez garage into a house built for humans. I usually had to drag myself to these seminars because I felt so out of place at them. Not because I didn't desperately need the information, cuz lawd knows I did, but because if any of my friends caught me there with a name tag pinned to my chest, discussing the power of gratitude in my little breakout group, participating in the call and answer: "Who's a wealth magnet?" "I'm a wealth magnet!" "I can't hear you?" "I'M A WEALTH MAGNET!" I'd never live it down. In other words, I felt above it all. Too cool for school. Snarkasaurus Rex. Sort of like people who love to travel (tourists) and love to comment (me) about how amazing a place would be if only there weren't so many tourists. Basically, I was obsessed with the idea of self-transformation, my own in particular, I was fascinated by concepts like the power of mindset, and I realized I wanted to be a life coach at the level of the guy up on stage instead of remaining the Book Lady for the rest of my life. But I was embarrassed to admit to any of it because I was afraid of what the people in my life would think. This was still back in the days when life coaching was regarded with the same highly questionable legitimacy as was (is?) psychic readings or hair-growth tonics. *What the hell is it anyway? Is it like therapy? Does it involve doing jumping jacks?*

Anyway, the event was being held by a coach I'd been following for a while but had never worked with before. I was on his mailing list, had read all his newsletters, and came to discover that he was a brilliant and captivating speaker. For some reason, he'd say things I'd heard a million times before and suddenly the light would go on, I'd be on my feet, fist in the air, sobbing with newfound understanding. "I AM a wealth magnet dammit! I am," sniff, "I really am." I knew he was the guy I needed to work with to completely transform my life, my business, and crack the code to making multiple six figures consistently, easily, happily, and hopefully while holding a fruity cocktail in my hand on a beach somewhere.

On the last day of the seminar, while we were all fully grasping the profundity of our own limitless potential, he pitched us two opportunities to work with him. One was a group coaching package where you'd gather in person a couple of times a year, get phone support, e-mail support, group cheerleading, etc., for $15,000. Then there was the big, fancy, no-nonsense yearlong package where you got to work with the master one-on-one. This option was for those of us who were really not screwing around, who were ready to completely transform our financial realities, and who knew he was the right mentor to get us there. This was me. This was exactly what I needed. This cost $85,000.

At the time I'd already invested thousands of dollars in getting coaching—private, group, anything, don't care what kind just help me get past my shit—and every time it was a major, terrifying financial stretch for me. Yet every time I worked with the right coach I got great results for a couple of reasons. First, because I'm an excellent coachee—I love to learn and challenge myself, I'm malleable, motivated once I make a decision, terrified of getting in trouble for not doing my work, etc. I also had officially reached my pain threshold for feeling at the mercy of money, and had tasted enough little victories to know I could blow the roof off the sucker and go as big as I wanted with the right guidance.

But $85,000, that was some serious cheddah! To even entertain the concept of someone like me getting my hands on that kind of money seemed impossible, as far-fetched as stopping by Saturn for a carton of milk on my way home. This was house-sized money. This was more than my annual income. This would get my friends to stop laughing at me and start intervening. Yet . . . because I'd just spent the past three days raising my frequency and my fist, and expanding my perception way beyond the limits of my present "reality," I wasn't thinking about what a delusional freak this guy was, I was thinking about how I could come up with 85,000 extra dollars.

And the moment I switched how I was thinking, when I went from *No way* to *There must be a way* in a flash, I suddenly realized what was perhaps the biggest obstacle that had been holding me back from making money for my entire life.

There are a whole bunch of tricks that will help you unearth your deep-seated, money-repelling subconscious beliefs, and I'm going to start with the most powerful, which is this: Hurl yourself into the fire. Run face-first toward your biggest fear. Take big, audacious action in the direction of your dreams and do not let the fact that you're wetting your pants stop you. For me, the combo of forking over such a gigantic chunk of change and the realization of just how big and visible I could/would get if I applied myself at this level launched me into an alternate reality. The possibility of the money and the success felt really really really real for the first time, and it freaked the Little Prince right out of me.

This is the feeling you're going for when you make a huge leap in your life: equal parts excitement and terror. And if you succeed at staying the course, one of the many glorious results can be that you'll freak your subconscious out so massively (remember, it's trying to keep you safely tucked away inside your comfort zone) that it will rise up, guns a-blazin', and reveal itself to you like a pheasant being startled out of a bush. This is exactly what happened to me. By thinking a thought I'd never thought before that was way outside my comfort zone, aka *I'm the kind of person who can manifest $85,000 for a coaching program and become gigantically successful,* one of my deepest, darkest beliefs that was hidden at the very bottom of my subconscious appeared before me, all covered in slime and seaweed, clear as day. And it was this: If I became a financially successful woman, my adorable father, who worked his whole life to provide and care for me, would be crushed, defeated, and abandoned because I would no longer need him.

As I waited in line to hand over my credit card and put down a deposit, I had an image of my sweet old dad, standing there in his yellow V-neck sweater that he was never seen not wearing, staring down at his tennis shoes with his hands in his pockets, at a loss for what to do or say. Even though he wasn't supporting me, my father's favorite method of showing me love, and feeling needed and valued, was to give me money, and I realized that I subconsciously believed that if I got rich, I'd be rejecting his love and basically stabbing him in the heart.

This realization was easily some of the most important information I've ever received in my life, aside from learning that Jeff Rumarez had a crush on me in ninth grade too. Once in possession of my heartbreak over dear old Dad, I was able to question, defuse, and rewrite my limiting, subconscious belief and grow forth in grand, new ways. . . .

## BUSTING YOURSELF TIP #1: BUM-RUSH YOUR FEARS.

Figure out something you can do right now that will take you a giant step closer to your goal of getting rich. Make sure it's something scary, something that you'd really rather not do because it's super uncomfy, something that makes you feel like you might puke, e.g., renting the massive space for your new handbag company, flying across the country and figuring out how to get yourself in front of the guy who's hiring for that engineering job that you're perfect for, cold-calling ten prospective clients, hiring a new full-time employee, etc. Notice any limiting subconscious beliefs that may get scared out of hiding as a result, and if you have anything come forth, write it down. Or, you know, have a meltdown. In public. Like I did. I broke down into such an unraveled state of sobbing hysteria in the middle of this seminar that the only reason I survived was that I didn't want to spend my last days on earth in Las Vegas. But afterward, I felt great. It was like hurling up something that really needed to leave my system. I felt lighter, relieved, like I'd been handed a permission slip to finally grow up.

Once you've uncovered your heretofore unknown unhelpful belief, take the time to feel whatever feelings come up. I mean it—pause, acknowledge, and let any sadness or frustration or heartache out of your system: *Damn you, limiting subconscious belief! I spent half a century eating clam chowder from a can at home instead of dining at the fancy steak house because of you!*

Let your feelings rip, but don't hang out there for the rest of your life. Your Little Prince was trying to keep you alive and loved, so once you've had your temper tantrum, focus on where you're headed, not on resenting the past.

Once you've discovered what's been holding you back and given yourself a chance to start releasing it, begin feeling into a new story using the specifics of what you've learned. For example, I visualized my father being so happy and proud of my financial success. I imagined myself telling him how much I love him, thanking him for being such an awesome role model, and felt him being relieved that I was able to take care of myself financially. Another thing that I did and still do is let him give me money. I'm so much more aware of how it lights him up, which then lights me up, and my newfound understanding of the energy in this exchange makes me receive the money with even more gratitude and love for my dad than I had when I actually needed it. He has no idea about any of this (um, Dad, are you reading this?) and that's not the point—this is all your stuff, these are the beliefs that you created yourself, it's about releasing the energy inside you, not about involving other people in your therapy session.

## BUSTING YOURSELF TIP #2: WATCH YOUR MOUTH.

If I say to you, "You can't make money because you're a moron," it conjures up a thought and a feeling in you, just as, "You are awesome, infinitely powerful, and I love you," brings up a thought and a feeling too. Your thoughts are the superhighway to the spiritual world, which is where Universal Intelligence is hanging out, filing its nails, waiting for you to place an order. And since words and thoughts are total besties—they share everything, finish each other's sentences, back each other up, and pass information and emotions back and forth like secret notes in high school—if you're broke or not where you want to be financially, you can be sure that your language could use an upgrade. Just like taking massive action can call forth buried beliefs, so can noticing what falls out of your mouth. Words are great truffle pigs to uncover your hidden thoughts and beliefs about money.

Luckily, the process of busting yourself on your words is pretty easy. You basically just have to make the decision to pay attention. Now that you've made the commitment to read this book and figure out your money stuff, make the commitment to become aware of your language. Make this your mantra: *Slow down and shut up.* Get practiced at taking deep breaths before you speak. This will give you the space to stop, notice what was about to come out of your mouth, and course correct if needed.

Paying attention to what other people say is another great trick (and, you know, kind of a good thing to do in general). It'll give you the chance to think: *Hmmm, is that what I sound like?* This is usually very enlightening because the people we hang out with most tend to share our own perceptions of reality, and hence tend to verbalize the same beliefs about money that we do.

Here are some phrases to watch for with others and yourself:

I want (= I lack)

I wish (but I'm not in control = disempowering)

I need (cuz I ain't got = lack)

I can't (obv)

I'm trying (but I'm not committed)

I hope (might happen/might not = lacks faith)

I should (but maybe I won't and maybe I don't wanna)

I don't know (spoken as truth, slams door shut on
    finding out)

Here are some excellent replacements:

I have

I create

I'm grateful for

I enjoy

I can

I choose

I love

Additionally, two words we need to be particularly stealth
about sniffing out are the words "I know."* Nothing slams

the door on further investigation and radical action faster than *Yeah, I know it's important to be aware of my thoughts. No need to explain—next topic!* They're very sneaky words because we tend to think we're rather impressive for knowing things, when in reality, no matter how much we "know," there are always more sides to the story, giant leaps of faith, and an infinite number of questions that could massively expand our awareness. Especially in the realm of self-helpery, where we often need to hear things over and over and over before they click, it's critical to stay wide-eyed and wondering.

The other thing "I know" does is shut us off from receiving information from Universal Intelligence. When we're so convinced by, and attached to, what our brains are telling us, we lose out on receiving this much deeper knowledge. What we're basically doing is acting like we're smarter than Universal Intelligence, the stuff that created all that is in our infinite Universe, meanwhile we can barely remember which day is trash day.

*IMPORTANT "I KNOW" NOTE: You have clearance to use "I know" when used as a confirmation of awesomeness, as in "I know I can make buttloads of money, I know I am a badass motherfucker," etc.

Which brings me to my next tip.

## BUSTING YOURSELF TIP #3:
## SHUT UP EVEN MORE.

One of my favorite sayings is: "A wise man once said nothing." I love this quote on so many levels because it reminds us that when we get silent, step out of the way, and listen to the big smarty-pants known as our intuition and the Universe, true wisdom can reach us. And flow out of us. And that so much of what falls out of our mouths is about *Look at me! I'm going to tell you five million awesome things about myself so that you will love me! I'm gonna make fun of myself before anyone else can so I don't feel stupid*–type stuff. Words are powerful tools for connecting with our fellow humans, to share with them information, love, hi-larity, ideas, chicken piccata recipes. The more you slow down and shut up, the better chance you have to make powerful choices, and the more space you have to catch yourself in the moment and ask: *Why am I about to say this?*

One of the best ways to blast past the noise in our brains and discover what's going on underneath is through medita-tion. Sitting in purposeful silence. Even if it's just for five minutes a day, if you do it every damn day it will make such a difference you won't believe you didn't sit down and shut up sooner. Set a timer, sit in a comfortable position, focus on your breathing, notice what thoughts come in and gently push them back out by refocusing on your breathing. I highly recommend keeping a notebook nearby to write down any thoughts that come through that you want to remember and investigate further. Ask yourself a question about something you're struggling with before sitting down, like, *What thoughts about money are blocking my flow?*

Another revealing exercise is visualization. Take five or ten minutes to imagine yourself living out one of the specif-ics of your desire for riches. Let's say one of the reasons you want to be rich is so you can take your family on a trip to

Madrid. Picture yourself there, notice how it feels, how it smells, where you stay, what you see, eat, buy, yell at the cranky cab driver about. Imagine what other people think of you taking this trip. Stay in the feeling and notice if any gnarly beliefs come up, anything about not deserving to travel or being selfish or *People are in dire need all over the world and you're spending your money whooping it up at the Museum of Ham?* Write down anything that comes up and question it.

## BUSTING YOURSELF TIP #4: HAVE AN "US" TALK WITH MONEY.

Whether you realize it or not, you're having a relationship with money. If you ain't got any money, it's because if you treated the people in your life with the same regard you treat money, you'd be dining on a Thanksgiving chicken for one every November. One of the best ways to find out how you truly feel about money is to write a letter to it as if it were a person. I personally found this exercise to be a real humdinger and have heard from clients and readers that they too realized they were acting like total fruit loops when it came to money. Back in the day, my letter to money went something along the lines of: *Dear money, I love you and wish I had more of you, but I resent the crap out of needing you. You're never there for me, I totally don't trust you, I feel dirty admitting I want you, but I get so excited whenever you show up. I worry about you all the time. I wish I didn't need you. You suck. Please for the love of God show up in huge quantities soon.* I had such a push/pull relationship with money, as do most people, it's a wonder I was able to bring in any at all. My energy was all about blocking it while trying to welcome it in at the same time.

Here are some snippets of letters sent in by readers to show you that you are not alone in your money madness:

> *Dear money,*
>
> *I feel confident and secure when you're here, and I like to spend you when you're around. I feel generous to others. But sometimes you leave without saying goodbye. You're like a lover who comes and goes on a whim, and yet I always want you back. It makes me feel resentful and frustrated. I get so scared when you go because I'm afraid maybe you'll never come back. It makes me feel bad about myself. Why can't you just enjoy being together?*

> *Dear money,*
>
> *I love you and respect you and try really hard to use you wisely, but I often feel like I let you down. Unless I work really hard I don't feel I deserve to have more of you in my life. I know all the wonderful things that we can do together: enjoy amazing vacations, bless my family, give to charities I believe in, and yet I often don't feel I deserve to have more of you in my life.*

> *Dear money,*
>
> *I love you and I'm scared of you. It would be amazing to have more of you but I feel weird admitting that. Like*

*it makes me a bad person somehow. I also don't know what I would do if I made tons of you. I feel like I would just give it all away because I don't know anything about investing so I'm probably blocking you from showing up so I don't have to look stupid.*

*Dear money,*

*I love having you around and I want to keep you safe so you can help me if an emergency comes up in my life. But I'm afraid if I have too much of you others may be resentful or my husband will try to take you from me. I don't have an education or skill set that will pay me enough to have as much of you as I want.*

*Dear money,*

*I really hate you. I hate that you have the ability to literally cause me physical pain when I look at bills. I hate that my stomach leaps into my throat whenever I look at my student loan balance. I hate that you have this much power over me. I actually would love to dedicate my life to helping people but I feel beholden to take jobs that I dislike so I can make more of you. I wish that I could have a clean slate with you. I want to come from a place of abundance and not one of fear, anger, and regret.*

I heard a story about a monkey trap that's used in certain parts of Africa and India that's a great metaphor for how we choose to hold on to our limiting beliefs about money. What they do is take a box, put a hole in it, stick a banana inside the box, leave it where the monkeys hang out, and wait. When a monkey comes along and sees the box, he reaches in and grabs the banana and gets trapped because his fistful of banana is too big to pull out through the hole in the box. If he wants to be free all he has to do is let go, and if he insists on holding on he will be trapped.

I can't remember where I first heard this story, but it's made the rounds in the personal development world for years and I'm pretty sure it's total BS. First of all, how would the monkey know there's a banana in the box? And second, how do they catch him once he's sitting there, stuck, holding onto the banana? Do they hang around all day in the jungle, smoking cigarettes and playing cards, waiting for the monkey with their nets at the ready? I went to one Web site that suggested that when they saw the monkey they quickly put him in a jar. A jar! Lame.

I've decided to use this story anyway because:

a. I could be wrong, it could be true.

b. It illustrates a point I'm trying to make really well.

c. The point I'm trying to make is that we make up these total BS stories and all we have to do is let go of them if we want to change our lives and be free, so what better story to relate it to than one that also might be total BS?

We choose to stay in our stories because we get what I call false benefits from them—we get to keep our identities as a broke person, we get to blame our brokeness on things outside ourselves (I don't have time, I have seven kids, the economy sucks, I can't find a pen to write down my to-do list with), we don't have to push ourselves outside our comfort zones and risk failing, looking like an idiot, losing money, changing and becoming different from our family and friends—the list goes on and on and it all comes down to this:

> You have to want your dreams more than you want your drama.

As we embark here on busting you on your limiting beliefs, I want to caution you against getting so wrapped up in processing your blocks that you don't take the action necessary to change your life. I've seen many cases where people get so obsessed with their issues that they spend years journaling, going to retreats, weepily deconstructing their inner selves as an excuse not to take giant scary leaps forward. So I want to encourage you to do both at the same time: Investigate your BS and take forward action. I want to reiterate that taking huge scary leaps into the unknown is the best way to scare your BS to the surface anyway. It's like a two-for-one deal—you make progress and you unearth your shit. The key is to keep moving forward when you uncover your deep-seated fears and beliefs, not retreat into endless self-analysis.

I'm not proud to report that when I had my big breakthrough about my dad at the money seminar, I did exactly what I just told you not to do—I didn't take immediate action on getting the $85,000 together and moving forward with my goal. I shrank back and focused on all my old fear, doubts, and worries instead of staying focused on how right this opportunity was for me. I hesitated, and instead of signing up and bravely leaping into the next chapter of my life, I snuck out of the conference room and went home. I'd love to blame it on the fact that it was an insane amount of money for me to come up with at the time, but it was my lack of determination and my fear that failed me, not the amount (I ended up manifesting that exact amount one year later to get coaching from someone else).

This is such a key point. When you get a hit on what's holding you back and realize what you need to do to move forward, act immediately. You are battling very deeply in-grained, and up until this moment, extremely successful limiting beliefs that have been your truths for your entire life. If you hesitate when you get a knowing hint, you give those familiar, limiting beliefs the time and space to take over again. Hesitation is the crack that all your favorite excuses will burst through, drown out your resolve, and sweep you back to the safety of your comfort zone. Listen to your intuition, trust Universal Intelligence over your fears, have faith that what you desire already exists, and leap like the mighty badass that you are. You can dooooooo eeeeeeet!

## TO GET RICH

Suggested Money Mantra (say it, write it, feel it, own it):
*I love money because money is always here for me.*

1. Write down the five most common limiting words or phrases you and the people you hang out with most use to talk about money.

2. Shut up, slow down, stop using them.

3. Meditate for at least five minutes every day. Before sitting down, ask the question, "What belief is blocking me from making money?" Write down any insights you get, question them, come up with a new story and repeat it to yourself as described in the previous chapter.

4. Come up with one superexciting reason that you want to make money and spend five to ten minutes visualizing all the details of it. Notice if any limiting beliefs come up and, if so, follow the drill in number 3.

5. Write a letter to money. Notice the key, most emotional limiting beliefs that come up for you and do the rewrite drill for them too.

6. Listen to your intuition during meditation, visualization, or just running around being you, and the moment you get a brilliant idea that would move you in the direction of your financial dreams, jump on it. Go for it like you've never gone

for it before. Leap like the largest leaping leaper ever. No-tice any crappy thoughts that come up while you're in mid-air, and rewrite them, but do not stop your forward motion in order to do so. The successful completion of this one exercise could land you in full-on badassery. Just sayin'.

Please fill in the blank:
I'm grateful to money because _____.

# CHAPTER 5

# THE HOLLERING OF
# YOUR HEART

I wrote the first *You Are a Badass* book while I was staying on a farm in northern California. The deal was I could have the entire seventeen-acre paradise, complete with beautiful sunny house and views in all directions, if I took care of their horse and two goats. I'm a little scared of horses (and don't you need a special license or degree or something to take care of an animal that large?) and knew nothing about goats other than that they can chew through cans, but I loved the place, and I love animals, and staying there ended up being one of my favorite chunks of time ever.

I'd spend my days sitting on the couch in front of the giant windows, typing on my laptop while gazing out at Diablo Mountain. The goats spent their days sitting on the porch in front of the sliding glass door, gazing at me, waiting in vain to be let inside. Sometimes they'd get up and chase the horse around the yard or run full speed into each other's heads, but for the most part they'd just glare at me with their weird goatly eyes, aggressively chewing their cud, insulted and un-amused by their outdoor-only status. Every so often, when they just could not believe I still hadn't gotten up and invited them in, they'd take matters into their own hands and hurl themselves against the glass or get up on their hind legs and pound it with their hooves.

One day while I was off in town shopping, I returned home after about five hours to find the horse standing in the drive-way by himself. Although he was truly one of the biggest horses I'd ever laid eyes on, he was also one of the neediest, and was rarely, if ever, more than twenty feet away from his goats.

"What are you doing out here all by yourself?" I asked him as I got out of the car, pausing to listen to the familiar sound of goat hooves banging against a glass door. My first thought was how strange it was that they'd be trying to get in when I wasn't home (they were equally as needy about me as the horse was about them). My second thought was *Holy. Fucking. Shit.*

I realized they weren't trying to get in. They were trying to get *out*.

In a slow-motion sprint, I ran up to the house, let myself in, shoved the goats out, and did my best to shut and barri-cade the newly compromised door. I then proceeded to stand frozen, with my hands over my mouth, uttering "Oh my God" over and over and over as I took in the sight before me. It was like witnessing the aftermath of a particularly debauched fraternity party full of amateur drinkers—epic, shocking, and so staggeringly horrible you can't help but look even though you really don't want to.

The goats had finally made the impossible dream come true by knocking the sliding glass door off its track and bursting through the screen, which subsequently closed on its own, trapping them inside with nothing else to do but completely destroy the place for five delirious hours. Their handiwork involved knocking over every single potted plant, smashing the planters and kicking dirt, planter, and plant debris in an impressively wide radius. They pulled the dish towel off the counter that I had glasses drying on, thereby shattering glass all over the place. Then there was the pooping and pissing party, which took place on every single piece of furniture and in every imaginable corner. They excreted their excrement on my bed, the white couch, the coffee table, the dining-room table, the bench in the hallway, and inside my shower. There was such an incredible volume of urine, in fact, I imagined that they somehow must have waved the horse inside so he could get in on the fun too. For their grand finale, they hopped up and down and knocked nearly every single piece of artwork off the wall onto the floor. I mean, who thinks to *do* that?

My first reaction was shock, but I have to admit, after that I was pretty damn impressed. They really did a great, thorough job. We could all learn a thing or two from their tireless commitment to detail and the pride they so clearly took in their work.

Here are some secrets to success that the goats modeled beautifully:

- Chewing, kicking, stampeding through any obstacles in their paths.

- Pooh-poohing the rules.

- Dreaming. Bigger than goats are told they can dream.

- Never taking no for an answer.

- Following their hearts no matter what.

- Not stopping until they reached their goal.

It opened up a whole new world for them, literally and metaphorically. They transcended their Outdoor Farm Animals status and became Creatures Who've Experienced Thousand-Thread-Count Sheets. They were forever changed. What this meant was that they became colossal pains in the ass, and more destructive than any goat has ever been, which is saying something. Drunk with power on their victory and newfound mindset that anything they desire is possible, they broke through the gate and started terrorizing the neighborhood on a regular basis. They began jumping all over people's parked cars, tried to break and enter any sliding glass door they happened upon, tore down bird feeders, obliterated gardens, and chased after small dogs, all the while maniacally screaming, yelling, laughing, and pissing wherever they pleased, like a pair of carousing psychopaths. I quickly got the gate fixed, patched all the holes in the fence surrounding the property, and covered my car in giant slabs of plywood to keep them off it, but the horse and I never looked at the goats the same way again. We were both kinda in awe.

......................................................................

Doubts, fears, and other people's rules are no match for a heart on a mission.

......................................................................

In order to become rich, you must connect to your desire for money with the passion of a goat who wants in off the porch. And the key to doing this is by getting clear on the specifics around your Why: Why do you desire this money? What will you spend it on? How will it feel to make it, spend it, and bask in the manifestation of your ever so important Why? Just wanting to get rich isn't going to cut it— there has to be meaning behind the money or else the second it gets hard or expensive or someone tells you you're high if you think you can get rich by selling your homemade ice cream, you'll slink back to your goat pen of complacency instead of doing whatever it takes. Start by thinking about what inspired you to pick up this book. How is more money going to add value to your life? How will getting rich change who you're being in the world? Which of your gifts are you the most excited to share in exchange for money? Where do you feel you bring the most value to your fellow earthlings? How does it feel to share your biggest, badassiest self with others?

If you're going to make more money, you need to get in touch with the emotions surrounding your incentive for making it, because emotions are what drive you to action. And if you're going to make the kind of money you've never made before, you're going to have to do a whole lotta stuff you ain't never done before, which will scare and challenge (and excite) the crap out of you. So you're going to want to be real fired up about getting rich and very clear about why it's so important to you. Here are the best ways to do that.

## GET REAL SPECIFIC

The average person is barely motivated enough to scrape together what they need to make a living with the occasional splurge on impractical, yet supercute, shoes thrown in here and there, let alone saddle up to bring in the kind of money that can change their entire perspective of the world they live in (i.e., from a frustrating place of limitations to an oyster of awesomeness). Don't get me wrong, every single person has the ability, but you need to have a big, burning blaze of desire roaring away beneath your fanny if you're going to take the risks, make the mental shifts, and stay the course until you reach your new, sparkly financial reality.

In order to inspire ourselves to make money, the exciting kind that we've never made before, we need to be . . . excited about it. And because money on its own is a meaningless pile of paper and coins, you're gonna want to get crystal clear about what the money is for, what it means to you, and how it makes you feel. This will be that fire for you. Vague aspirations lead to vague results; specific aspirations lead to kicking ass. There are a couple reasons for this:

1. Specifics allow the Universe to fulfill your order.

    You wouldn't go to a deli and order a sandwich by saying, "Hi, yes, I'd like a sandwich, please." You'd order the specific kind you want: "Roast beef, mayo no mustard, pickles, lettuce, tomato, on a roll, please—actually not that roll, can I have that bigger roll over there?" And you would, hence, receive the specific sandwich you ordered. And it would make you happy. The Universe needs details too. It will respond, it always responds, but if you just focus on how awesome it would be to make more money, you may receive ten bucks instead of the tens of thousands that would make a significant change in your life.

2. Specifics create emotions, and emotions give us the no-nonsense determination to do whatever it takes to reach our goals.

    For example, feel into the different levels of emotional drive in the following scenarios:

    You're ready to get rich and you decide to make an extra fifty thousand dollars. You think about how exciting this will feel, imagine your bank account with all the new zeros in it, feel the power of being able to manifest that kind of cash and picture yourself doing victory laps around your house. While all of this is great, it doesn't have the same emotional charge as something more specific, like: deciding to make fifty extra thousand this year, forty of which you'll use to make the renovations on your kitchen that you've been talking about for years. You've cut out pictures of awesome kitchens from various home design magazines and put them on a vision board that you look at every day, you've priced the entire project out down to the cost of the cabinet knobs, you imagine yourself joyfully cooking your ass off while surrounded by dear friends and family. You feel the space, smell the food, see yourself feeding the people you love, and you experience the satisfaction of knowing you created it because you can create anything. The other ten thousand dollars you've decided you will give to your sister to help her launch her new dog grooming business. You love your sister, and seeing her overcome by joy that she can live her dream, and that you have helped her, makes you want to do cartwheels. Knowing you are the kind of person who has the means to help others gives deep meaning to your life.

You want to feel so turned on by the thought of this money that you're leaping out of bed in the morning to the sound of trumpets, rather than slowly putting on your socks thinking, yeah, that would be cool. Here are some examples gathered from my readers that will hopefully help you get clear on your Why. I love being rich because:

- It makes me feel confident and powerful knowing I did what it took to stop being broke and get rich.

- The more money you have, the more freedom you have with your time. I want to be able to let my nanny go, and hang out with my kids more.

- I can contribute thousands of dollars a year to charities that help save animals.

- I can spend my money on going to the movies, buying clothes I love, going out for dinner (which I love to do more than anything), instead of having to use it just for bills, necessities, etc.

- I can buy great gifts for people and finally take my family to Portugal.

- I can see myself in the best possible light, I'm being the best version of myself, I've let myself be all I want to be.

- I'll be an inspiration to other women like my daughters and women in struggle, specifically those who feel trapped in abusive relationships with men.

- I'll sleep peacefully at night knowing I'm in the black. Right now I'm not sleeping so well due to stress.

- Early retirement—woot!

The other reason to fall in love with your desires for riches is because love is your greatest weapon against your limiting subconscious beliefs. Love is all consuming, it muscles its way in front of all other thoughts and emotions, including all the fear, doubt, and worry buried in your subconscious mind. Think about it—when you fall in love with a person, thoughts of them overpower everything else. Love is like a drug that alters your ability to participate in logical thinking, to focus on anything other than the object of your desire, or to have interesting conversations. "I know, there are a lot of flies in this restaurant. Bob, the guy I'm in love with, had a fly in his house once."

Same thing goes for when you fall in love with the specific reasons you want to get rich. Any coping mechanisms, compliments of your limiting subconscious beliefs, that might try to keep you right where you are will be no match for your burning desire for greatness. Any fears and beliefs that you'll become a sellout or a greedy fathead like your awful Aunt Sally will be drowned out by the harps and chirping of bluebirds taking up space in your head and your heart. We fall in love with very specific things and people, so getting mighty clear on the details of your impending richness is critical.

## ALIGN WITH YOUR TRUEST YOU

After the goats raped and pillaged my home, it took me several days to get it back to normal. I also wound up spending a thousand dollars getting the hood of my (brand-new, thank you very much) Audi replaced after they kicked away the plywood and tap danced all over it. Yet I couldn't get mad at them. Not only were they ridiculously cute, but they're goats.

It's in their nature to destroy, to hop on things, to wake up in the morning and think, *What shall we fuck with today?* It would be like getting mad at my dog for barking at crows or mad at my ninety-year-old Italian father for refusing to eat anything but Italian food. Ever. Ninety years of uninterrupted pasta. They're just being true to who they are.

All living things come hardwired with certain traits and characteristics that are part of our nature. Meaning that these things come naturally to us, they're what we're meant to do and they're how Universal Intelligence flows through us best. Birds gotta fly, fish gotta swim, the guy next to me at the coffee shop right now gotta eat his granola with his fingers. When we push against who we naturally are, we feel stress, things don't progress easily, we beat ourselves up for getting crappy results, everything is an effort. This is why listening to what everyone else thinks you should be doing (including your scaredy-cat self) is so deadly. You wind up trying to force your way through life, which can make sitting on your butt at a desk all day utterly exhausting if it's not what you want to do. Meanwhile, when you listen to your heart and connect with who you're meant to become, you have energy because you're in a state of flow, things happen more easily, opportunities land in your lap, you're turned on, inspired, engulfed in a sea of brilliant ideas. Yes, there will be challenges and things will blow up in your face, but learning experiences are different from wasting your life pushing a boulder up a hill.

Pay attention to the things you're drawn to, the things you're good at, the things you lose yourself in, the things that make you stand up and say, "My foot! I can't feel my foot!"

because you've been sitting in the same position for hours, totally engrossed. Allow yourself to be pulled by your heart instead of pushing your way through a thick fog of shoulds. So often we discredit the things that come naturally because we've bought into the idea that success needs to be difficult, or that if something comes easily to us, it must come easily to everyone, and therefore isn't worth pursuing in any serious sort of way.

I have a friend who toiled away for years at a job as an advertising executive that he loathed. He's an old buddy of mine who is, among other things, a brilliant performer, pant wettingly hilarious, and the main reason all my parties back in the day were so damn fun. He'd do things like wait by the front door and announce each new arrival through a bullhorn made out of a toilet paper roll: "Presenting Catherine Atkinson, of the once lived next door to Jen Atkinsons. Please make her feel welcome by complimenting her on her excellent posture." He'd organize impromptu talent shows, music jams, and have willing guests sit for him while he painted their portraits on crackers with spreadable cheese.

Not surprisingly, he was constantly getting asked to help organize and host everything from bat mitzvahs to Thin Lizzy tribute nights, and while he enjoyed the work and did it well, at the same time, it was, you know, work. He believed, however, that he couldn't charge for this type of thing. First of all, he had fun doing it, which for some reason meant he couldn't get paid. Second of all, he felt weird asking for money from his friends. Lastly, he felt that anyone could herd people around an event and crack jokes on stage. What value did he bring? He went on for years basically working two jobs—the one he got paid for and hated and the one he loved that made his eyes look like two pissholes in a snowbank from exhaustion. Then one fateful day, he saw a professional MC at some corporate advertising event he had to go to for work. The guy was not only getting paid, a lot, but he was nowhere near as hilarious, charming, or adored by the crowd as was my pal.

I'm pleased to report that this guy was so profoundly bad, and pissed my friend off so massively, that he finally got over his attachment to can't, shouldn't, and wouldn't, and started charging for his brilliant MC services. He also asked everyone he worked for to spread the word about his new profession, and today is in high demand as a professional MC. By having the audacity to follow his heart instead of his fears, he was able to quit his hateful job and now spends his valuable time on Earth getting paid to be the life of the party.

......................................................................................

Your heart is the most powerful muscle in your body.
Do what it says.

......................................................................................

## TAKE A STAND FOR THE AND

While taking this dictation from your heart and getting clear on your Why, make sure you don't fall prey to the deadly either/or syndrome. Here's the deal: We live in a fear-based society that totally gets off on cautioning us, on reminding us how difficult life is, on warning us how hard it is to make money, on holding us back lest we bite off more than we can chew, on screaming "Look out!" instead of "Rock on!" As a result, we've bought into this idea that it's better to limit ourselves than to stretch, and we've developed this fun-free either/or take on what's available to us: You're either doing what you love or making money, you're either a good person or a rich person, you can either help the world or you can help yourself, you can either go on vacation or pay your car loan.

Y.A.W.N.

Instead of looking to where you can cut back, save, and play it safe, look to how you can expand, grow, and start acting like a badass who's in control of your own life:

Have a big fancy career AND be a great mom.

Be a good Christian AND make tons of money.

Travel the world AND run your own business.

Be at your desired weight AND eat chicken wings.

Get a time-share AND save for your old age.

As you take the time to imagine your life as the biggest, boldest, and most authentic expression of the you that is you, don't be a cheapskate when it comes to taking inventory of what lights up your heart. Act as if you live in an abundant Universe (which you do) and have the ability to create whatever financial reality you desire (which you can), and that by doing this you'll be sharing the most magnificent version of yourself with the world (which you will).

## OPEN WIDE

I know I just spent several pages screaming about the importance of specifics, but you must also stay open to allow Universal Intelligence to deliver what you need, and the thing or person or opportunity that makes your heart sing may be in a different form than the one you were thinking. Once again, we must trust that the Universe knows more than we do, and if we white knuckle it over things like, "I see myself making $12,500 by selling three extra cars at my dealership this month," you will block the very same riches that the Universe is trying to hand you via a film company renting out your showroom to use in a movie. Your job is to envision your life with all the specifics you can muster up so you can get all emotional and excited and take inspired action. Then you hand the rest over to the Universe. Otherwise known as surrendering, this is a key factor in consciously managing your energy to create an awesome reality for yourself.

IMPORTANT NOTE IF YOU'RE IN THE "I DON'T KNOW" CAMP: If you're like, *I have no freaking idea what my heart desires or what I want to do with my life other than I don't want to buy my groceries at the dollar store anymore,* here are some things you can do right now:

1. Take action on what you do know. If there are bits and pieces that you are sure of, that feel totally right, focus on those instead of waiting until you've got the entire picture figured out. For example, if you know that you want the freedom of working for yourself, you love drawing, you're happiest when you're around animals, you want to help people, start with these pieces and act on them. You could volunteer at the local animal shelter and see who you meet and where that leads. Or start a business making drawings of people's pets. Or assist someone who helps people overcome trauma by working with horses. Once you start taking action you'll be able to discover more things you like, more things you don't like, and a clearer picture of what you desire to do will begin to form. Taking action leads to answers, mulling ideas around in your head forever leads to indecision and grouchiness.

2. Stop saying how clueless you are about what to do with your life (what you focus on you create more of) and talk about how excited you are to be filling in the pieces.

3. Make sure you're not pretending you don't know what you want to do when you actually do know, but you're scared. *I don't know* is different from *I can't make money doing what I love, I'm too old, people will think I'm an egomaniacal fathead for wanting to be a model, etc.* Roll up your sleeves, study those who've gone before you, decide you're unavailable to live your one and only life treating your dreams like they're not as important as your fears, demand of yourself

that you figure it out and make it happen. We have, after all, figured out space travel and how to make jam out of a cactus; you can figure out how to flourish doing what you love. Don't waste your precious gifts, and life, drowning in doubt.

Nobody else can want you to grow into your gloriousness for you. You have to be serious as a heart attack about creating an awesome life in order to crowbar yourself out of your comfort zone and make it happen. You've moved mountains before, I know you have, and it's because you really really desired to be, do, and have whatever it was that you desired. Maybe you asked someone on a date who was "out of your league," faced your fear of speaking in public, started your own business, gotten a job you were "unqualified" for, raised children, or moved across the country with nothing but five bucks in your pocket, a thermos full of hot cocoa, and a dream. When your desire is strong enough, nothing will hold you back. So . . . how badly do you want to have all the riches required to live all the life you can live? Spend some time hanging out with your heart, get clear on your almighty Why, and let your fears know they ain't the boss of you.

### SUCCESS STORY: IF SHE CAN DO IT, SO CAN YOU.

*Here's an awesome story from a client of mine, Anita, 32, who got real specific, trusted Universal Intelligence, and put more faith in her Why than in her Are you freaking kidding me's and manifested $75,000:*

I was thinking about where I wanted to take my life next, and I assumed that what I needed to do was quit my job and start a new and exciting chapter. It had been something I'd been thinking about for a long time.

But every time I focused on that goal, it just didn't feel right. Finally, I realized that in order for me to really be ready to quit my job, I needed to close out some key household debts. Our mortgage was nearly paid off and the car loan wasn't too bad, so I determined that if I could just pay off those two loans, I would feel okay with quitting my job—especially being the primary wage earner in our family. The sum of these debts was about $75,000. Okay, so now I have a goal to find $75,000!! How the heck am I going to find $75,000.

I thought, *this is crazy! What gives me the right to expect that this is even possible? I'm not going to find a pile of money lying around, and I'm also not going to be able to take on another job or sell something that would earn that amount.* I started feeling sort of silly (and maybe not worthy?) about my goal. I felt stuck.

After about a week of whining about it, I stopped the fear crap and started focusing on the number 75. I meditated on the number 75, I wrote 75s all over my journal, I BELIEVED that something would work out . . . and then . . . nothing was happening. Geesh! I laid in bed one night and thought that there must be something I'm not seeing. There must be somewhere I haven't looked for the money. I reminded myself that all that I desire is already here . . . somewhere.

And then I remembered that way back in 1999 I had received as a gift some stock for participating on an advisory board of a tech start-up. Hmm, now that the company had gone public, I wondered what it was worth. The stock info was buried somewhere in our home office files and, miraculously, I found the file easily the next morning. I did some research to find out whom to contact about these stock shares. I called the phone number of the management company to understand the value and how to sell them. I had no idea if they were worth anything, but I had to give it a try. The fund manager was extremely helpful and walked me through the process of selling the shares. I asked her what the value would be worth since it was a gift initially valued at about $200.

And guess how much it was worth now?

Are you ready for this?

Yep, $75,000. On the freakin' nose!

I nearly dropped the phone when she told me. I am still in shock and also extremely excited. Pardon the crudeness here, but THIS SHIT WORKS!

Don't give up on your dreams!!!!

## TO GET RICH

Suggested Money Mantra (say it, write it, feel it, own it):
*I love money because I love living an awesome life.*

1. Write a fantasy "Day in the Life." What would a typical day in your life as the richest, happiest, and most successful version of yourself look like? We can rattle on all day about what we don't want, but being very clear about what you do want usually takes a bit more doing, especially since you're looking to radically change your life—you've never experienced or owned many of the things you're seeking, so how the hell can you know? This is why it's so important when you're writing this to come more from feeling than from your analytical brain. Give yourself time while you write it, do it stream of consciousness and see what you come up with. Write it in the present tense, as if money weren't an issue, think what would be so fun, not just reasonable, what would make you most excited to give back or leave as a legacy, go to town.

2. Once you've written your day in the life, write down the five strongest emotions you feel when you read it.

3. Do the numbers around your day in the life, get an idea on the page of how much this life of yours is going to cost.

4. Boil down your day in the life, taking the most exciting details of it and combining them with the cost and the feelings

they bring up so you can create a mantra. Don't worry about fitting everything in, just the most compelling parts. Then write a five- to ten-sentence mantra, something like, *I love making three hundred thousand dollars a year as an interior designer. It's so exciting working with clients who are smart and who appreciate me, traveling the world and discovering new ways to be creative. It makes me feel happy and invigorated and like my heart could explode. I'm so grateful that this affords me the opportunity to live by the beach in San Diego with my soul mate and that we go surfing every day. . . .*

5. Read your mantra every night before going to bed and feeeeeel it.

6. If you're not sure what you want to do, make a list of the things you do know, be as specific as possible, and write down five action steps you will take right now to move yourself in that direction.

Please fill in the blank:
I'm grateful to money because _____.

## CHAPTER 6

# YOUR MENTAL MONEYMAKER

There's a great story that the actor Jim Carrey told on the *Oprah Winfrey Show* about how he used his mental mightiness to manifest $10 million and a successful acting career. He always knew he wanted to entertain people, discovered he had a face made out of Silly Putty at an early age, and got his first gig at a comedy club at fifteen. After a series of ups and downs that included dropping out of high school to help support his family by working in a factory during the day, and then getting laughs—and getting boos—in comedy clubs at night, Carrey wound up broke and living in a van with his aforementioned family. He eventually moved to Los Angeles to pursue his dream of becoming a famous actor for reals. He said that even though he was broke and jobless, he'd imagine having directors interested in him, visualize people he respected coming up to tell him they liked his work, he'd focus on thinking things like, *I am an awesome actor, powerful people in the industry are out there waiting for me,* and it made him feel better even though he wasn't exactly getting mobbed by fans at the hardware store or anything.

He also wrote a check out to himself for $10 million, dated it three years in the future, and put in the memo that it was for acting services rendered. He carried this ratty thing around with him in his wallet for years as he got more comedy gigs, TV gigs, and movie gigs, none of which made his career, or his finances, take off the way he was hoping they would. But he kept believing anyway, kept visualizing himself using his riches to care for his family and fueling his feeling of success, kept working his ass off and, to make a very long story short, just before the date he'd written on the check in his wallet, he landed his role in the movie *Dumb and Dumber* and got paid $10 million for acting services rendered.

We all have the choice to think what we want to think, and to take responsibility for the fact that our thoughts create our financial realities. Universal Intelligence is like a giant ear with a glass pressed up against your mind, listening to your thoughts—otherwise known as its working orders—so it can get down to business and help you create whatever you set your mind to.

........................................................

**If it's on your mind it will soon be in your lap.**

........................................................

I love this story about Jim Carrey because it illustrates what it takes to master the mindset of wealth:

- Get clear on what you desire, get specific—What is your purpose? How much money do you desire to make by expressing this purpose? By when will you make this money? Why do you desire it, what is it for?

- Hold the vision of this reality in your mind with a no-nonsense resolve and a relentless sense of purpose to make it real.

- Fall so madly in love with your vision that it's no match for any limiting subconscious beliefs that pitch a fit and try to stop you.

- Have faith as firm as a firefighter's fanny and wide-eyed gratitude that it's already yours, even if it feels like it's taking for freaking ever. Never lose faith. Ever.

- Take action with hell-bent-for-glory purpose and faith.

Carrey's story also speaks to one of the most common objections I hear when discussing your mindset's role in making money, which is: *What if your financial reality depends on the actions of other people? How can your thoughts control what other people do?* I hear this a lot from those who rely on other people to hire them, like actors, corporate types, plumbers, caterers, babysitters, leaf blowers, etc., as well as people in multilevel marketing businesses who rely on the people in their down line to bring in the money they then get a percentage of. If you think about it, all people rely on other people to buy their products and services, to strengthen their investments, to pay the cover at their gigs, or to spare them a dime for a cup of coffee. Money comes to us from Universal Intelligence through other people, so no one gets to use the ole *I can't control other people* as an excuse for staying broke.

My first experience with the power of mastering your mindset was just as beyondo, and, dare I say, magical as Jim Carrey's $10-million check situation. It happened when I was working with my very first private coach, the one who helped me start my online business helping writers complete their book proposals, called writeyourdamnbook.com, and who was also helping me hone my chops as a life coach. At the time, I'd worked with a couple of private coaching clients of my own here and there, and had basically tripled my annual income with writeyour damnbook.com. Tripling my income was hugely exciting, but wasn't gonna have me flying first class anytime soon, considering people working the drive-through at the Friendly Fajita made more than I used to make. I wanted to bring in the kind of money that would make me feel like a different person. I wanted to feel large and in charge, like I could make whatever I decided to make, like I was free, flying, fucking around no more.

My coach asked me to come up with an amount that, if I totally hustled and busted my ass, I could make in a week with writeyourdamnbook.com. She said not to think about it, not to do the math, not to figure in what other people were charging, but to just let the amount come in intuitively. The number that popped into my head was five thousand dollars in one week. Until then, the most I'd made in a week was probably one or two grand. It was terrifying, but I was excited and dare I say a little bit cocky about my ability to make it happen.

"Great," she said. "Now double it."

Once I came to, we put together a plan of action. I would work privately with three people and help them write their entire book proposals for three thousand dollars each. I was also going to sell one of my already existing thousand-dollar group coaching programs, which would bring my total for the week to ten grand. I had no idea how I was going to talk three people into spending that kind of money for the pleasure of working with me. All I knew was that I was going to make that ten thousand dollars because I was officially unavailable for any other outcome.

Then we did the energy work, and I got clear on things like:

Why do I want the money? *To feel in charge of my life and to feel free, like I'm not at the mercy of money.*

What will I use the money for? *To pay off my ten thousand dollars' worth of credit card debt. I hate being in credit card debt, credit card debt is a giant sucking thing.*

What will I do to make the money? *Sell three private book proposal–coaching packages and one spot in my group coaching program. As well as stay open to any suggestions the Almighty Universe tosses my way.*

When will I make it by? *This question was a doozy because I knew, in order to pull this off, I had to go at it like it was a life-or-death situation. I knew I'd have to be so unflinchingly focused on making this ten thousand dollars that you could pelt me with rocks, cut off my electricity, and let a gorilla loose in my living room and I'd still stay the course until I was victorious. I didn't know how long I could sustain that kind of no-nonsensery, so even though my coach said I had a whole week to make the money, I decided I would make it in two days.*

So I'm on the phone with my coach and we're figuring all this out and I'm all psyched up and freaked out and ready to make money my bitch and suddenly this idea pops into my head out of nowhere. There was a man who I'd worked with a year ago, he was actually my very first private life-coaching client. I hadn't heard anything from him in at least a year, but maybe I could reach out to him to see if he wanted to work together again. He wasn't a writer, but maybe he wanted to do some general life-coaching stuff? Almost as soon as the idea popped into my head, an e-mail popped into my in-box. From *him. I had heard nary a peep from him in over one year and the moment I thought of him, he appeared in my in-box.* My hair is still standing up over this one. In his e-mail he said he wanted to start working together again, what kind of life-coaching packages did I have and how much did they cost?

To make a long story maybe actually come to a freaking end around here, I sold him a six-month private life-coaching package for twelve thousand dollars and ended up selling one of my three-thousand-dollar coaching packages to a writer the next day, which meant I made fifteen grand in forty-eight hours. Which for me at the time might as well have been a million dollars in eight minutes.

There are a couple of things I want to point out about this story. One is that the money came to me through a different person in a different way than I thought it was going to. Part of working with Universal Intelligence is doing everything you know how to do but staying open to ideas and opportunities that "come out of nowhere." Your job is to get your energy aligned, be dead serious about bringing this money in, and take all the action you know how to take. Universal Intelligence's job is to move what you desire toward you in whatever way it sees fit.

The other thing to point out is the mindset shift I had to make in order to charge my client twelve freaking thousand dollars. I adored this man, I'd had such an excellent experience working with him before, and I really wanted to help him. The last time I worked with him I was charging something like twenty-five bucks an hour for my coaching services. My twelve-thousand-dollar coaching package put me at three hundred dollars an hour. At least. Sending him back an e-mail with that price tag on it was one of the scariest things I've ever done, because part of me, the part I was in the process of shedding, felt like a bad person, like who the hell did I think I was to charge that amount? This part of me felt like if he wrote me back and told me to go to hell, I would respect that. But the part of me that was ready to play big, that had the audacity to think I could make ten thousand dollars in forty-eight hours as well as do anything else I set my mind to, that understood the different energy behind charging three hundred dollars an hour versus twenty-five dollars an hour—this part of me felt my price was right on. I'd been coaching and studying coaching for years at this point, I knew I was good at it, and charging that amount of money, as terrifying as it was, was also totally exciting, empowering, and felt, energetically, where I was meant to be. I knew I would show up as the best damn coach I could possibly be, and when he wrote back immediately and told me to sign him up, I realized he was ready to stretch himself and play at that high a level too.

By being clear about where I was at, and aligning with money at that high a frequency, I offered him a chance to participate at the level I was at too. And I will tell you, it was so much money for both of us that we both kicked so much ass I'm still feeling it. I became Super Coach and he went out and manifested a multimillion-dollar business deal within the next few months.

While it's true you can't control other people (except through physical force and manipulation if you're lame that way, of course), you can control your thoughts and actions, and that is what you need to focus on to shift your financial reality. The people who complain and blame—blameplain?— stay stuck: "The economy is swirling down the toilet bowl right now—of course my new electrical business is tanking! How the hell are my thoughts supposed to control that?" Instead of upgrading their mindsets and demanding of themselves, and the Universe, that things start to change around here, they insist that everything is out of their control. They hand all their power over to their circumstances instead of taking responsibility and changing their lives themselves. Then there are people like Jim Carrey, parked on Mulholland Drive, overlooking the City of Angels, with nary a prospect in sight, all giddy with belief and gratitude that he is rich and famous as he sits there, eating beans out of a can with a plastic spoon in his crappy car.

You can have your excuses or you can have success. You can't have both. Whichever outcome you train your mind on dictates the reality you see before you. Some people have much bigger struggles and obstacles to overcome than others, but we're all given the same choice as to how we perceive our reality. There are people raised in extreme poverty, with little to no education or prospects or support, who believe they can create riches anyway. They focus their attention and actions on getting wealthy, instead of on the negative aspects of their circumstances, and go on to make millions, even billions. There are also people who are born rich, who get educated at the best schools, who have fancy connections, vocabularies, and monogrammed pillowcases, and who wind up living on the streets. Success is not about your circumstances, it's about who you're being. People have gotten rich doing and selling everything and people have also gone broke doing and selling the same things the exact same ways.

## YOUR ATTITUDE HAS THE WHEEL

Here are some surefire ways to harness the almighty power of thought to get as wealthy as you wanna:

### FOCUS

What you focus on you create more of. This is such a simple concept, but it bears repeating over and over, and I will repeat it over and over, because it's so damn powerful and so immediately flung out the window because we're so attached to "the way things are." We don't want to believe that things could be that easy, to give up our right to feel sorry for ourselves, to relinquish the comfort we take in knowing a thing or two based on our past experiences, and to, erm, take responsibility for our lives instead of being like, *I can barely afford to buy a bag of Fritos, how am I supposed to hire someone to get my Web site up and running?*

Meanwhile, we use our mighty power of focus all the time and we don't even realize it—we use it to create unhappiness in our lives via our dear pal worry.

................................................................

**Worrying is praying for stuff you don't want.**

................................................................

Because you're focused on the worst possible scenario and all the reasons you can't possibly have what you want, and there are lots of emotions and specifics and faith involved, you create more of what you don't want over and over with expert precision. But the beautiful news is, if you're one of those people who are particularly skilled at worrying, this means your focus muscle is in great shape, and all you have to do is choose to focus in a different direction.

Let's say, for example, that you're twenty thousand dollars in debt, you've got twelve children you need to support, you hate your job, and you live in a shoe. Choosing to focus on these aspects of your reality and freaking out about them will do the following:

- Anchor in the belief that your life sucks the big one.

- Trigger thoughts about how hopeless your situation is.

- Activate emotions of terror and sadness and loseriness.

- Inspire you to get in the fetal position.

Now, 'twere you to make the conscious choice to shift your focus and view the very same situation in a new light, such as: *When I needed twenty thousand dollars it was there for me, which means if I need money again it will be there for me again, I'm so grateful I have money coming in from my job, and believe that since I got a job once, I can get an even better job, because I am clearly very hirable, I am surrounded by love and family, and I live in a shoe— how cool is that?!*

This new perspective allows you to:

- Anchor in the belief that you have things to be grate-ful for.

- Trigger thoughts about how blessed you are.

- Activate emotions of joy and hope and excitement.

- Inspire you to get out there and make more awesome stuff happen.

Changing your focus to the positives of what you have and what you desire changes your attitude and raises your fre-quency so you can align your energy with, and open yourself up to, everything you need to change your life: the moneymaking opportunities you didn't notice before, the people you can help and the people who can help you, and the ability to visualize a bigger life for yourself. It also sends thoughts of what you desire, not what you fear, out to Universal Intelligence, so it can start moving it toward you.

Here's another important aspect of focus:

........................................................................

It's impossible to focus on one thing and see another.

........................................................................

Which is why when you're trapped in worry, you not only keep creating more of it, you literally can't see all the other possibilities that are surrounding you.

For example, once when I had a hankering for a tuna fish sandwich, I went to the pantry to grab a can and found my craving crushed under the realization that I was tunaless. The little blue can of albacore was nowhere to be found (insert sad trombone sound here). Right before I left the pantry in defeat, I thought to myself, *I KNOW I have some damn tuna*, so I kept looking and suddenly, lo and behold, right in front of my face, there appeared two cans of tuna. The thing is, the cans were red, not the usual blue (I switched brands, you see), and because I was looking for blue, not red, I did not see them.

I'm sharing this lunchtime suspense thriller with you because it illustrates how often we miss out on the golden financial opportunities, life-changing connections, and heart-opening experiences that we crave because we're stuck in old ways of thinking, believing, and hence, focusing.

.................................................................

When you focus on your past, you are blind
to your present.

.................................................................

You are the master of your reality, and your perception is manning the control knobs.

## EMOTION

When it comes to ramping it up to rake in the dough, any positive thoughts you're choosing to think that lack emotion are flaccid, useless, and windbaggy. Affirmations like *I love money, money flows to me effortlessly, I am a badass at making money,* if buried beneath the heavy sigh of *as if,* are a big fat waste of everyone's time. Just thinking something doesn't mean you believe it—it's only when gargantuan positive emotions are involved that thoughts are able to access their superhero powers to create new expansive beliefs, fearless actions, and as a result, exciting new realities in our bank accounts and other areas of our lives.

Because we are both spiritual and physical beings, we've got a whole slew of things going on in the realm of the unseen—thoughts, beliefs, intuition, imagination, emotions, etc., all of which affect our physical realities here on Earth. When you're in emotional pain, for example, you cry, your face gets all tight and weird looking, maybe you sometimes even puke you're so upset. When you're excited, your heart speeds up, your body tingles, and you run into traffic, drag a stranger out of their car, and kiss them all over their head. Our emotions are the motivating kicks in the rear that alert our bodies that it's time to take action and make a thought a physical reality. Just like the table lamp takes electricity and transforms it into light, our bodies take thoughts and turn them into results. In order for this to happen, in both cases, a switch needs to be flicked. Emotions are the switch.

If you find yourself swirling in a whirlpool of suckery it's because of this chain reaction: You think something that triggers an emotion that then causes you to act in a way that keeps you caught in a loop of frustrating results. Let's say, for example, that your complaint of choice is "I'm broke." It's your go-to whenever faced with the possibility of fun or growth: Want to go to the movies? *I can't, I'm broke.* Want to go out for dinner with exciting, successful people who will inspire the crap out of you and very possibly change your life? *I can't, I'm broke.* Want to buy a magic pill that will make you rich, young, and hilariously funny? *I can't, I'm broke.* Instead of rallying and accessing your imagination, your will, your *I'ma figure it out because this is important to me, oh yes I am!* muscle, the emotions of despair and hopelessness keep you in a state of constantly re-creating your ho-hum "reality"—you can't see past your present situation, you've blocked your ability to imagine, you've chosen victimhood. I mean, with that sad-sack thought of *I'm broke* looping through your head, you barely have the energy to bend down and pick a nickel up off the sidewalk let alone leap bravely into the unknown. To break free from your rut, you must make the choice to think something else and slather it with emotion.

..................................................

The thoughts, beliefs, and emotions we don't consciously reject, we unconsciously accept.

..................................................

Awareness is the key to freedom. When you pay attention to how you're thinking and feeling—*Hmm, when I say I'm broke it makes me feel like crap*—you empower yourself to make a better choice, to instead think thoughts that light you up like a yard in Queens at Christmastime.

The best way to be as mighty as you can be is by getting crystal clear about, and extremely attached to, your Why. Employ the muscle of imagination, envision yourself in the life you desire to live, feel the feelings that having this money and this life call forth. Conjure up the emotions associated with your purpose for making money and cling to them like a baby monkey.

As James Allen says in *As a Man Thinketh*: *Thought allied fearlessly with purpose becomes creative force.*

Here's some other helpful things to know about emotions:

- Emotions don't like to share their space. If you're sick of feeling scared or sad or frustrated, focus all your energy on building up the opposite emotion. Compassion drowns out hate and vice versa, excitement drowns out fear and vice versa, belief drowns out skepticism and vice versa. I was at a funeral for a friend from college, sitting in a row with all my old pals, and a very old lady sat down in front of us, wheeling an oxygen tank behind her. One of my friends looked down at the row of us and mouthed "nitrous" and we all fell apart laughing, our sadness suddenly, and temporarily, nowhere to be found.

IMPORTANT EMOTIONS NOTE: We are feeling creatures, we are meant to experience, not deny, our emotions. Ergo, it's not about being all yippy skippy every moment of every day and never ever feeling sad or angry or freaked out. Expecting yourself to feel only positive emotions is not only impossible, but will most likely make you feel like a failure instead of like a normal human. Feel what you feel, have a temper tantrum, shake your fist in the air and curse thy enemy's name, lie facedown in your driveway and weep, let your emotions live large and then . . . make the decision to move on. It's when we wallow in our negative emotions that we let them hold us back. Experiencing them, however, is healthy and critical to releasing them.

- Love is the undisputed heavyweight champion of the world. Love beats the crap out of fear, hate, jealousy, worry, insecurity, irritation, grouchiness—it's stronger than all of 'em. If we all just spent our days focusing on strengthening our love muscles, lawd the changes we'd see. But for you, dear soon-to-be-rich person, practice viewing everything in your world, and I mean everything, even your backed-up septic tank, with love and appreciation and behold where it gets you. Fall madly in love with your purpose for making money and you will be unstoppable.

## STRETCH YOUR IMAGINATION

One of the coolest gifts we have to help us on our road to riches is our imagination. Imagination is the mental kitchen where we cook up two types of make-believe:

1. The kind where we take ingredients from our surroundings and experiences and mold them to our liking: *I see myself living in a house just like the Nelsons' next door, I see myself showing my kids what's possible by creating my dream life, I see myself buying drinks for everyone down at the Drunken Tomato, etc.*

2. The kind where we take ingredients from the spirit realm and bring them to life: the invention of space travel, the idea for the first skyscrapers, the creation of the electric can opener, etc.

Imagination is awesome because it doesn't rely on physical circumstances, our five senses, or anything our parents told us about how important it is to have fresh breath if you want to succeed in life, for validation. It's through our imagination, not our current version of the "truth," that we're able to play with the infinite possibilities that are available to us. Anything goes when our hearts and our imaginations are at the helm.

Stretching your imagination is critical if you want to radically change your life, because we're asking ourselves to picture our dream lives from the "realities" we currently exist in. *Well, I'm fifty-eight, I work in a shoe store and support my wife and two kids, and you're telling me I could own the hotel of my dreams on Lake Tahoe and teach people how to fish all day? There is no way I can see that happening. Ever.* We don't dare think too big because it seems ridiculous—I mean, we can talk all day long about how making a few million a year would be awesome, but to actually set about making that amount with the unwavering knowledge that it is happening dammit and not stopping until we get there is a whole other banana. It takes some serious noive to even allow yourself to entertain the idea, let alone go for it with the conviction that it's going to happen. When something seems so big, so magnificent, so out of reach, it requires you to believe it's possible before you've got any proof that you could ever pull it off. In fact, it usually requires you to ignore a lifetime of proof that you probably can't pull it off. It's much easier, and more "realistic," to pare down the dream, shoot for what's reasonable, ask for less.

........................................................................

Riches come to those who believe anything is
possible even when all signs point to No Way in Hell.

........................................................................

When I was toiling away back in the day, making about thirty grand a year, it occurred to me that after spending four decades trying, and failing, to become financially successful on my own, perhaps it would be wise to get some help. This is when I decided to hire my first coach, who is the one I mentioned in the beginning of this chapter. At the time I was freelance writing, knitting, etc., but I was also facilitating/coaching groups of women entrepreneurs on getting their businesses off the ground (ironically, I was great at helping other people figure out their lives). I met my coach through this entrepreneurial group, and she charged me seven thousand dollars to work with her privately. Which, if you're math oriented, feel free, otherwise I'm just gonna go ahead and say that this was a terrifying percentage of my annual income. It was also twice what I paid for my car, cost more than all my furniture, clothes, and frozen burrito purchases put together, and it was more than the amount I still had left to pay on my student loans. In our culture, there are a few words to describe this kind of behavior: Irresponsible. Delusional. Full-goose bozo. Because what I also did was go even deeper into debt by maxing out the credit cards I had, as well as the new one I somehow miraculously applied for and got.

............................................................

If you want to change your life, you must be more
available for the ridiculous than your reality.

............................................................

For me, making money was about freedom and options. Getting my ass out of debt, traveling the world, moving to a house where I could entertain more than two people at a time were all great incentives, but what really got me rolling up my sleeves every morning was my determination to become a different person. I wanted to be someone who created whatever I set my mind to instead of someone who settled for what I could get. If I got an idea about a trip I wanted to take, a cause I wanted to invest in, or a giant hat covered in fur and feathers that I wanted to buy, I wanted the feeling of freedom that came along with knowing I could do it or have it. I wanted to be in control, not at the mercy of, the circumstances in my life.

Regardless of where you presently find yourself, if you spend time hanging out in that imaginary space of big possibility, relishing the details of your dream life, where riches flow to you no problemo, you can start to embody what success feels like and connect to the meaning that making money has for you. By imagining and envisioning yourself where you want to be, you start to get excited, you start to develop belief, faith, and hell-bent-for-glory purposefulness. These feelings are key to getting yourself to do what it takes to make your dreams manifest in physical form. These thoughts also inform Universal Intelligence that you are not screwing around, and it sets about the process of flinging everything you need to manifest your dream in your direction—including such incredulities as coincidences, intuitive hits, and opportunities straight out of the clear blue sky. Your role is to keep your mindset strong, open, and ready to receive. And to do a whole lotta stuff you've never done before.

Especially stuff that scares the living crap out of you and hurls you outside your comfort zone.

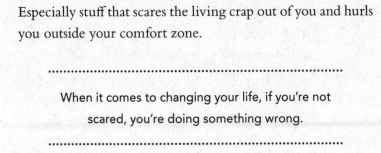

When it comes to changing your life, if you're not scared, you're doing something wrong.

When I decided I definitely wanted to work with this coach, my desire to change and to no longer be a victim of my rickety "reality" inspired me to switch my thinking from *I ain't got the seven grand to pay her* to *I will find it dammit*. I focused all my energy on my desire to work with her and my belief that she could help me change my life. She not only specialized in helping women make money, but she walked her talk. At the time, she was making multiple six figures with her coaching business, but she had once been so broke she had her electricity turned off and one evening had to turn away the pizza delivery guy for lack of funds on her credit card—I mean, this woman turned away *a pizza*. Talk about having been through it.

What was far more important to me than her fee or my debt or the very real possibility that if I didn't pull this off I'd be sharing an address with my mother, was my mindset. I had gotten to the point in my life when I was so freaking sick of being broke, of feeling trapped, of knowing I could be doing so much more with my one and only life that I made the no-nonsense decision that no matter what, I would seize all opportunities that resonated with me to learn about money, to make money, and to do what it took to get rich. So when I met a coach who I felt could help me, instead of looking at the price tag and my bank account and thinking, *Oh well, not exactly a match made in heaven, maybe I'll call around and see if anyone's up for a beer,* I hustled and demanded of myself that I find the money for her seven-thousand-dollar fee.

This is the critical moment for us all—the moment the Universe places before you exactly what you need and asks you to rise to the occasion. Are you going to stick with low-frequency thoughts like: *I'm broke, it says it right there in my bank account. The end.* OR will you stretch, raise your frequency, and find your way to *My financial situation is temporary, it's not who I am, it's where I am, money is all around me, I'ma find me some and make this happen.*

........................................................

What you can and can't afford is all in your mind.

........................................................

If I told you to go out and make two thousand dollars in the next twenty-four hours, if your mindset wasn't in the right place you might give it a shot for a few hours and then succumb to thoughts of *I can't because I'm too clueless/lazy/busy, I tried everything and it didn't work, there is nothing I can do, not that's legal anyway, etc.* However, if I chased you down the street swinging a sock full of nickels over my head threatening to beat you with it if you didn't increase your income, you would open yourself up to possibilities that, before you made the decision that it absolutely had to happen, you literally could not see (taking out a loan, selling your car, approaching important, intimidating people for help, etc.). Where there's a will there's a way; we just prefer to pretend there isn't a way so we don't have to take responsibility and do the uncomfortable stuff required to grow.

---

An excuse is nothing but a challenge that you've given your power to.

---

The big secret to getting rich isn't so much about brilliant plans or hard work or good connections or amazing timing as it is about thoughts and emotions. Our thoughts and emotions catalyze not only our actions, they also supply all the ingredients for the Cocktail of Creation:

Belief

Clarity

Focus

Faith

Urgency

Decisive action

Tenacity

Gratitude

When you've got all these pieces in place and working together, ain't nothing you can't do.

## DETERMINATION

I got writeyourdamnbook.com up and running a couple of months after signing on with my coach, and to my great glee, I started making money almost immediately. The business angle made sense for me: I was a successful, albeit broke, freelance writer, I was tapped into a national network of women entrepreneurs thanks to my job coaching the ladies on their businesses, I was tech savvy enough to handle the Internet and computer requirements, and I was serious about getting my act together.

To my great horror, I also became one of those unforgivably cheesy salespeople hocking their stuff online. I knew that supersmart online marketers had tested the methods I was using over and over, and that I was making money right away because I was following their wise lead but . . . why did it have to involve, among many other horrifying things, posting on the World Wide Web for all to see, a sales banner with a big picture of me on it, looking professional and oh so together in my business casuals? I begged my coach to tell me there was another way to do things, and she just looked at me and asked, "Do you want to be broke and cool or rich and cheesy?"

........................................................

You can't experience new lands from the confines of
your comfort zone.

........................................................

The Universe will always send you what you need. It wants you to succeed, it wants you to grow and blossom and shine, it's the law of nature fer fek's sake. But just like the emperor penguin that has to carry his one egg eight trillion miles through perilous icy terrains to his hatching grounds, or the giant sequoia tree that needs intense heat from raging forest fires or some scary insect to crack open the cones that house its seeds . . . when it comes to birthing new life, the Universe wants to know just how serious you really are.

For the first few years of my business, I lived a dual life. I was terrified that my friends and fellow musicians (I'd been in rock bands for years) would stumble upon my goobery online marketing materials. I also lived in fear that my new book proposal clients would discover pictures of me in my punk band, Crotch, wasted and rocking out wearing a hair bikini, and politely ask for their money back.

For years I tossed and turned in the midst of this major identity crisis, but my determination to make money was more important than my discomfort over what I had to do to make it. If I had to look cheesy, I did. If I had to spend even more money on hiring tech people to help me, I did. If I had to go to endless amounts of networking events and hand out my business card, I did.

..................................................................

How determined you are determines your outcome.

..................................................................

Deciding to get rich means you put that decision above all else (except doing illegal, amoral, revolting things for money, of course). You need to be ruthless with yourself because you're not only growing a new moneymaking mindset, you're battling a whole lot of subconscious beliefs about money that you've probably never faced before. Any chink in your armor will offer your old conditioning an opportunity to take over and steer you off course, which it will do so quickly you won't know what hit you. You can't:

- Be weird about the fact that you not only desire to get rich, but that you're going to focus everything you've got on making it happen.

- Make sure everything is perfect before starting. There's a fine line between perfectionism and procrastination. Get the damn Web site up, the business cards made, the headshots taken, whatever—get yourself in the position to start bringing in money and deal with fine-tuning it later.

- Be precious about getting rid of all the distractions in your life. Distractions are like unwanted hair. Get rid of one and another will sprout up somewhere else. Get rid of whatever is most easily dealt with, and as far as the rest go, learn to stay focused on making money in spite of them. There is never a lack of great excuses or reasons to shift your focus and slow your roll. Stay determined, stay focused.

- Whine about how little time you have or how nobody around you is supportive or that you're already

working forty hours a week, *how the hell am I sup-*
*posed to do more?* Take responsibility for the fact that
you created everything in your life via your thoughts,
beliefs, focus, actions, and energy, and that you have
the power to shift your mindset, raise your frequency,
and create new things that will serve you better. Get
out of victim mode and into badass mode and be diligent about your mindset.

- Need to know exactly what you're doing before moving forward. Get practiced at taking the next step that
  feels right. There is no greater teacher than
  experience—you will get all the answers you need as
  much by falling on your face as you will by knocking it
  out of the park.

- Get advice from people who aren't farther along
  than you are. We tend to want to involve our old pals
  and people we feel comfortable with when we're
  pushing ourselves into a new financial zone, but if
  you really want to grow, you need to hang with people
  you can learn from, who know what they're doing, not
  just with people you feel comfortable with. Taking advice from people who are nowhere near where you
  want to be is one of the best ways to stay right where
  you are.

If you stick with it and start seeing some real results, everything, including your subconscious mind, will start to
shift.

## SUCCESS STORY: IF SHE CAN DO IT, SO CAN YOU.

*Katherine, 52, shows what having unshakable belief in yourself, and your pal money, can do:*

I've always been able to make good money. I've always believed I was good at making money and that has been a self-fulfilling prophecy. I can make money even when I'm not trying to. I started off as the lowest clerk in a financial services company, making about $15,000 a year, which was enough because I didn't spend a lot, but I worked hard and quickly moved up. I ended up as a vice president, making over $500,000 a year. As I started making more money, I took each raise that came and put half of it into savings, which was matched by the company, and retired very comfortably at age 40. Even after I retired, I started a gardening hobby, which soon became an income-producing business for me. I had no intention of doing that, my gardening business just seemed to evolve on its own. Making money is natural and easy for me; I see opportunities everywhere and am not afraid to jump in and see what happens.

I think believing that you can make money, that you are worthy of it, is most important. It's one area I've always believed in and not struggled with.

I always applied for jobs I wasn't sure I was capable of doing and then worked hard to figure out how to do them. Fake it until you make it. Act as if you know what you're doing and work your ass off until you do.

> If you believe you are capable of making money, you will, even when you don't try.
>
> Believe that you are worthy of financial freedom. Do something you love and then all you ever have to do is be yourself to succeed. If you sell something you love, then you just sell love, not a specific product or service, and that will show.

## TO GET RICH

Suggested Money Mantra (say it, write it, feel it, own it):
*I love money because it comes when I call.*

1. Write down what your Whys are for getting rich and give three reasons that each one is stronger than your fear.

2. Come up with three ways that you can fall more deeply in love with your Whys and do them every day. (Example: If your Why is *To take care of my family,* you could look at a picture of them every day, repeat the affirmation *My family is happy, healthy, and living abundantly because I'm a bad-ass at making money,* cut out pictures of the specific things you'll buy to take care of them with, and look at them every day. Stuff like that.)

3. Notice three things about your financial life that you're focusing on in a negative light and make the conscious choice

to shift your focus. (Example: *My bank account is a cavern-
ous pit of emptiness and sorrow* becomes *My bank account
is wide open and ready to receive.*)

Please fill in the blank:
I'm grateful to money because _____.

CHAPTER 7

# FAITH AND GRATITUDINAL GOLD

Imagine that some sort of Grand Pooh-Bah Master of the Universe came down from the heavens and informed you that all the riches you desired were in a warehouse down the street, and were totally 100 percent guaranteed to show up in your life, if you kept diligently working toward them: the money, the dream house, the thriving new business, the killer speaking career, your foundation fund to help the homeless, your mortgage payments, the certified, authentic tube top that Pat Benatar wore on her *In the Heat of the Night* tour that you saw on eBay, all of it.

How would you show up in life if this was the case? If you weren't distracted by feelings of doubt and worry niggling away in the back of your mind that maybe it wasn't going to happen for you after all?

You'd probably be more relaxed, more excited, you'd enjoy your work more—tweedily twee twee—you'd be more playful, positive, generous, grateful. You'd say things like, "When I get my boat I'ma let you drive it!" you'd invest whatever terrifying amounts of money you needed to into your business, you'd doodle "Me + the Universe = 4ever" on all your notebooks, you'd leap into new exciting/terrifying opportunities with a grateful expectation of victory, recover from mistakes more quickly, your words would be mightier, your swagger would be swaggier. Basically, you'd be psyched.

The person I just described has the mindset of someone who's wealthy, they've got all the fixins we've been talking about throughout this book so far. I also just described the mindset of someone who has unshakable faith in themselves and the Universe.

> **Your fortune is in your faith.**

Faith is required if you're going to upgrade from rickety to rolling in it because faith is the part of us that dares to believe that an unseen, unproven, and often proven otherwise, brand-new, and awesome reality is within our grasp. Without faith, aka belief in miracles, what would be the point of trying to create anything new and grand? We'd take one look around us and be like, *Alrighty, so, I reckon this is as good as it gets. . . . Check, please!*

Faith is the rocket that you ride into uncharted territory to get to your wildest dreams. And it needs to be mighty sturdy because you're flying through some crazy stuff, much of which is trying to knock you off course. The life you're determined to create depends on your rocket not falling apart. You're up against not only your own bonkers beliefs about money, but you'll most likely have people hurling their crappy fear, doubt, and worry at you too like a bunch of wild monkeys. Your faith must be fierce, fiery, not fuckin' around. You must believe that everything you desire really is available to you and that you possess all the tools, power, and permission to manifest it. Here's how having faith helps you get rich.

- Faith helps you give How the heave-ho. You created the life you're presently living by doing what you know how to do, and by being the person you know how to be. When you make the no-nonsense decision to get rich, you may not see any solutions or opportunities to make this new kind of money no matter how hard you look. This is because you're so busy focusing on what you think the How should look like that you can't see the new, unrecognizable How that the Universe is excitedly wagging in your face. Faith shifts your focus off the past, your old ways of doing things, and opens you up to new opportunities, new Hows, that will create a new reality.

    For example, when I was a struggling freelance writer, I decided I was going to get a part-time job that required getting dressed, leaving the house, and collaborating with other people. I didn't know what this job looked like or how I was going to find it, all I knew was that I was serious about making more money, helping other people, and having a reason to brush my hair.

One day a friend told me about an entrepreneurial think tank that helped women launch their own businesses. The old me would have instantly passed up this opportunity for fear of spending the money to join only to sit there, week after week, looking like a boob with zero ideas for a business. Yet even though it cost a lot of money for me at the time, and I had no idea how it could lead to me making any money, something about it just felt right. I was hell-bent on changing my financial situation, and since this opportunity involved leaving the house and hanging out with other people who were investing in getting their shit together, I forked over the money and joined up.

As I sat there listening to all these women brainstorming their ideas, I still had no idea for a business of my own, but I realized I'd be awesome at helping them figure out what to do with theirs. To make a very long story short, I asked the lady running the group if she needed any help facilitating, she hired me, I began my first foray into coaching, which led to me starting my own business as a coach, which led to me making mad money, which led to me sitting here writing this book.

If, instead of taking a leap of faith, I'd focused on my fear of wasting my money, of looking like a boob, of not yet seeing how those meetings would lead to me getting rich, I very possibly would be writing a book on Ten Easy Tips for Declaring Bankruptcy instead of a book on how to get rich.

You created the financial reality you're in right now by doing what you're doing how you're doing it— buying into your present excuses and limitations and working at the same old same old. If you're serious about creating a new reality, you must do different things and think different thoughts. Faith allows you to release the need to know How it's going to happen, to trust that the way will be shown, and to take action before having all the answers laid out before you.

- Faith raises your frequency. When you trust that your riches are on the way, instead of biting your nails over the *what-ifs* and *how the hells*, you shift your emotional state from doubt and fear to excited expectation. This shift raises your frequency, opens you up, and makes you aware of people and opportunities you weren't seeing before. This higher frequency also gives you the huzzah to take action on these new, unknown opportunities when they present themselves, instead of running screaming in the other direction, no matter how terrifying or expensive or *are you freaking kidding me* these new opportunities are (and trust me, they rarely come in any other form).

- Faith helps you shape shift. In order to become the new, richer you, you must relinquish your attachment to your present/old identity: *I'm broke, I hang out with other broke people, and we do broke things together. We believe we are X (noble, stuck, safe, screwed, etc.). We love our broke tribe and do not ever want to break it up.* Instead of focusing on what you risk losing when you grow, faith helps you focus on, and believe in, all you have to gain.

- Faith strengthens your relationship with Universal Intelligence. When you have faith enough to say, "I may not know exactly how I'm going to double my income, I just know that I am," you are trusting that the path to riches will be shown to you. Instead of expecting yourself to have all the answers, you're leaping into the unknown fully trusting that Universal Intelligence has your back: *Here I comes U Dawg, I know you're gonna catch me!* Your past and present knowledge of reality is being tossed aside for something that doesn't "exist" yet. If you didn't have faith that the Universe had something awesome in store for you, was there for you, and was, you know, smarter than you, you wouldn't let go of your present truth.

- Faith strengthens your self-confidence. If you're badass enough to leap off the edge of your present reality into the void, is there anything you can't do? The answer: No. Nothing.

- Faith strengthens your abundance mindset. Faith in the unknown and the miraculous removes your focus from what you lack, and homes in on infinite possibility. What you focus on you create more of. Hence, faith = abundance mindset = you're gonna need some bigger pockets.

Let's put faith into the context of stand-up comedy because it's a great metaphor for the sort of grit it takes to put yourself all the way out on the edge. If you lob a joke out into the audience and all you hear is crickets, it's just you up there with nowhere to turn, sucking on stage for all to see. You might as well just go ahead and do it naked to complete the nightmare. But when you nail a joke, all eyes are on you, all the laughter and glory is yours. It's thrilling, it's terrifying, it's all or nothing, and it's all you.

When you go big and take the scary leaps you need to take to change your financial sitch—hire an expensive stylist, enroll in beauty school, write your book, buy a castle and turn it into a disco—you're up there on stage with no idea what's on the other side of those blinding lights, free-falling through space. But here's the great news: If you nail it, party time! If you bomb, you now know what didn't work, so when you go out there and give it another shot, you get to do so with more info. Taking a leap of faith is a win/win. Treading water in your comfort zone for the rest of your life is a snore/yawn.

Faith, like all other facets of our mindset, is a muscle. The more you use it, the stronger it gets. The bigger the leap, the stronger your faith muscle needs to be. Staying steady, focused, and fixated on your faith when the poop really hits the fan marks the difference between those who are successful and those who fail. It's usually right after we think we literally cannot take one moment more of the uncertainty or the waiting or the pressure or the disappointments—*Holy hell-balls, are you trying to kill me over here?*—that the big investor comes through, or the counteroffer is accepted, or the soul mate walks through the door.

> A test of faith is like playing chicken
> with the Universe.

The Universe wants you to grow and bloom into the most glorious version of yourself. Growth happens through friction and challenge, and the lessons we learn through these experiences. Because the Universe is so excited for you to be all you can be, it is going to send you all the learning experiences you need: *Here's a flat tire on your way to your wedding! Here's a hurricane and a flood the day you open your new business! Here's nowhere to park when you're late for the job interview of your dreams!* When you have faith that everything happens as it's meant to, you open yourself up to receive the lesson, to stay the course until you're successful, and to not totally lose your shit.

In the midst of the particularly trying lessons and growing experiences, you have to hang in there like your life depends on it. With the really big stuff, very often you're required to get to the point where your faith is the only thing you've got left, because you've gone so far out to the edge that anything familiar or safe or rational isn't even a blip in your rearview mirror anymore. It's like flying or surfing or tripping: You have to focus on your faith and surrender to the cosmic rock tumbler because your only other option is to freak out and crash.

.........................................................

**Badassery comes to those who take risks.**

.........................................................

I recently had an offer from a production company to option the rights to one of my books. The offer was good, but we were haggling over one critical percentage and neither of us would budge. I wanted more, they wanted to give me less, and no matter how much we rearranged and tweaked other parts of the contract, this one point always just sat there, staring at us with blank eyes, the dead cow that wouldn't move.

I loved these people, felt they really understood my writing and my sense of humor, and was so psyched to work with them. When they said the dreaded words, "This is our final offer," and that damn percentage had yet to go up, I had to take a big ole leap of faith and pass. I didn't want to, we didn't have offers from any other production companies I was anywhere near as excited to work with, but the percentage felt low and I knew I'd be resentful if I took it. I had to have faith that an even more awesome offer was right around the corner and that my decision was solid, instead of freaking out about *what the hell did I just do, I just passed up the opportunity to have someone make a TV show out of my book while I lie around getting hot stone massages and count my money.*

Consciously keeping my focus on my faith was a challenge, I ain't gonna lie, but I did. I kept reminding myself that, of course, the deal I desired was on its way, I kept envisioning this deal, kept feeling into it, kept being grateful for it. I'm thrilled to report that their final offer was like Cher's never-ending final tour—they came around the following week and offered us what we asked for and now we're all happily moving forward together. I never would have had the strength to pass, stay the course, and wind up in this awesome situation without dear old faith.

At the end of this chapter I'm going to share some of my favorite methods for developing faith muscles so firm you could bounce a quarter off them. But now I want to spend a moment talking about the granddaddy of all personal workout coaches: gratitude. Whether it's strengthening your faith or your beliefs or your frequency or your thoughts or your relationship with Universal Intelligence, gratitude is one-stop shopping on your road to mightiness.

Unlike almost anything else, gratitude puts you in close contact with the spiritual realm. Gratitude, above all other thoughts, unites you with Universal Intelligence because you're basically matching your frequency to the frequency of the Universe via thoughts and feelings of love. Think of it like this: Let's say you live in a neighborhood with lots of kids and you bake a batch of cookies and hand them out. Some kids are so wrapped up in their play that they wolf them down without giving it much thought, some kids whine about wanting seconds, but there's one kid who shows deep appreciation. He's grateful for the cookie, for the gesture, for your big ole heart, he helps you clean the kitchen, refill your bird feeder, set up your iPhone. He's the kid who gets as many cookies as he wants and gets to lick the bowl. He's met your energy of giving with his energy of gratitude and his high-frequency response opens him up to receive more of that same energy from you as well as someone else.

......................................................

**Wealth appreciates for the appreciative.**

......................................................

Gratitude allows you to raise the energy you meet each situation with. When you're grateful for the lessons in challenging situations instead of feeling pissed off or put out or sorry for yourself, you raise your frequency and open yourself up to receiving more high-frequency experiences instead of repeating crappy old ones. Resentment attracts more resentment; denial keeps you stuck in the same place. But gratitude gets you out of the loop of lowness, opens you to new possibilities, and sets you free.

Let's say you're unemployed and you're driving to a job interview and you get into a car accident. Now you've missed the interview, lost the potential income and you're going to have to go deeper into debt to get a new car. I'm all for cursing and kicking tires and bursting into tears and getting the rage and frustration out of your system. This isn't about denying or suppressing your feelings, but it is about choosing to perceive your life in a powerful way. Even if you have no freaking idea what the lesson is in this situation, once you've had your temper tantrum, be grateful that it happened. You are in one moment in time, stranded on the side of the freeway, suddenly surrounded by shattered glass and traffic cones, and you have no idea how this situation is going to play out in the scope of your life. You could discover years later that it saved you from taking a job you would have hated instead of getting the one you now love, you could fall in love with the EMT who shows up on the scene of your accident. Or you could finally wake up and decide to do whatever it takes to get rich because having your car totaled was the final straw that inspired you to face your money issues and go whole hog to change your life. You can choose to be a victim to your circumstances or take responsibility for how you choose to perceive them.

........................................................................

**You can't see the silver lining through victim goggles.**

........................................................................

Have faith that you and the Universe have created everything for your growth and be grateful for it. No matter what. Get practiced at making gratitude your go-to, notice the eight trillion things around you at all times that you can be grateful for, and feel into the grateful expectation for all the things coming your way. The good, the bad, the ugly, the salsa stain you just got on your new white shirt, become a gratitude machine for all of it.

················································

There is no lack of things to be grateful for if you
remember to pay attention.

················································

If you're feeling frustrated and upset by your lack of income, spending some real time on gratitude is critical, especially if you feel like you're doing everything right—if you're
clear on your specifics, hauling ass, taking big risks, making
scary sales calls, paying people money you're scared to spend
to help you get your Web site up, and still . . . no dinero.
WTF? If you've got everything right, but you're dropping the
ball on being grateful, you are most likely pushing the money
away out of desperation for this freaking money to come in,
already. Desperation repels, gratitude attracts. When you're
desperate, you're stuck in the worry that the money's not
there and that you need to get it rather than knowing that it's
already here and there's no need to get anything. Remember,
money is currency and currency is energy. When you switch
into gratitude mode and focus on feeling grateful for all you
have and all that's coming your way, even if there isn't any
money anywhere in sight at the moment, you strengthen your
faith that the money will be there for you and align yourself
energetically with this belief, and you will start manifesting
the very things and opportunities you're grateful for.

I have a friend who's an interior designer. At the beginning of every year she figures out how much money she'd
like to make, what it's for, gets all in a tizzy about it, and then

she drives around her town and looks at all the houses, seeing each one as an opportunity to realize her dream. She obviously doesn't decorate every house, but she uses this exercise to anchor in the belief that there are countless houses and people who could use her services, who she could help and who can help her in return by paying her. For this she is deeply grateful, her faith is rock solid that, of course, she can have what she desires, and every year she meets her goal. Even if she doesn't have one damn client at the beginning of her little driving tour, she is grateful for all the clients that she knows the Universe is sending her.

It's like when you're on a plane and you take off on a drizzling, dark, depressing day. You look out the window at the gray sky, the sad little houses below getting misted with rain, then you head right into the dark clouds themselves. It's black and bumpy and scary and then— ta-da!—all of a sudden you pop out on top of it all into blue sky, fluffy clouds, and sunshine. The sunshine and fluffy clouds were there all along, you just couldn't see them from your perspective.

I don't care how insane or hopeless your situation appears to you right now, because it's not the truth, it's just what you're experiencing at the moment. There's an entirely different and sunny reality out there waiting for you, all you have to do is make the decision to blast through your own storm clouds of fear, doubt, and worry, stay in grateful expectation with unshakable faith that the sun is there even though you can't yet see it, and stay the course through the turbulence until you reach the other side.

## TO GET RICH

Suggested Money Mantra (say it, write it, feel it, own it):
*I love money and am grateful every day that it's surrounding me with its glorious goodness.*

1. Take five things in your life that frighten you, bum you out, irritate you, find reasons to be grateful for them, and write them down (and feel this gratitude, don't just give it lip service).

2. Make a list every evening before bed of ten things that you're grateful for.

3. List five reasons you have faith in yourself.

4. List five reasons you have faith in the Universe.

5. Give comes from abundance, get comes from lack. Place your focus on abundance and strengthen your faith by giving away money every day for twenty-nine days. Give as little as a nickel or as much as you can in whatever way you can. Do it secretly whenever possible.

6. Faith requires patience. All seeds have a gestation period and it's up to the Universe, not us, how long that period is. Getting all uptight and freaked out doesn't make it go any faster. Put three things in place to help yourself stay patient while keeping your faith strong. Here are some options: Practicing deep

breathing anytime you feel yourself starting to freak out, re-peating a mantra like "It's acomin', I can feel it!" Soaking in the feelings of how it will be once it arrives. Get superspecific and have these tools at the ready: What you focus on you create more of so focusing on impatience = lack = pushing it away. Choose what to focus on to strengthen your faith and patience and you will be victorious.

Please fill in the blank:
I'm grateful to money because _____.

# CHAPTER 8

# DECISIVE ACTION: THE CHOICE OF CHAMPIONS

I'm obsessed with this movie called *Touching the Void* about these two guys who climb some gigantic mountain that's never been summited by humans before because it's like the death star of snow and wind and icy forlornness. But they're into it, and they go and they summit and it's all high fives and *Woo-hoo we did it* and *I think I can see my house from here* and then, on the way down, of course . . . blizzard.

I watch a lot of these types of extreme survival movies where people have to eat each other's frozen bodies after a plane crash or cut their own arm off when a boulder lands on it and traps them in a canyon, but *Touching the Void* is high atop my list because, holy crap, what happens to one of the guys . . . I mean, just when you think things can't get worse they get so much worse you find yourself screaming "Oh my God!" out loud even if you're watching by yourself.

I'm not going to give away all the details because I really

want you to see it, but I am going to talk about the ending, because this guy is served one colossal shit biscuit after another after another after another, and his mindset is the only reason he gets out of there alive (you know at the beginning of the movie that he survives, btw, so no need to thank me). He has to traverse an endless expanse of frozen glacier that could, at any moment, crack open beneath him and send him spiraling down into a giant, bottomless crevasse. Then, once he's off the glacier, he has to stumble through an impossibly jagged terrain of boulders, all of which he does with a broken leg, a face that looks like a pepperoni pizza from frostbite and sunburn, frost-bitten fingers, frostbitten toes, no food, no water, no sun-glasses (so snow blind), covered in his own excrement, AND he has a really bad song stuck in his head.

He's trying to use his ice ax as a crutch, which doesn't really work, so he winds up slipping and falling and banging his mangled leg on rocks nearly every single step he takes, weeping and hollering in pain each time. But he never gives up, he just hops and falls and screams his way back to base camp, which, by the way, may or may not be deserted by the time he finally gets there. His team may have packed up and left him for dead. This agonizing journey seems to go on for nine hundred years, and if you're like, *Wait, is she describing my journey with trying to make money?* listen up because there's a lot of good stuff here that will help you escape the icy forlornness of your empty bank account.

The first and most important thing this climber did was to decide that he was going to live. This might seem like a no-brainer, the instinctual will to live and all, but . . . have you decided to live? I mean really live the way that you know you'd love to? If you're serious about getting rich enough to live your life to the fullest, you have to decide to do it with the tenacity of a man facing life-threatening and unbeatable odds with a really bad song stuck in his head. Because the second something goes wrong or gets hard or costs a lot of money or time, if you have decided lite instead of decided for reals, the second the going gets tough you'll be pulling out your favorite excuses, scripting convincing soliloquies on why quitting makes excellent sense, and weighing your options: *Well, if I just give up and lie here, I reckon I'll be frozen solid in a couple hours, won't feel a damn thing after that, and then I can gaze up at the stars until I slowly slip away and the birds start picking at my tore-up leg.*

You have to have a 10-ton gorilla of no-nonsense decidedness breathing down your neck to do what it takes, plow past your fears and subconscious hell nos, and leap into the unknown. Deciding means there is no plan B, you've yanked in your one foot out the door and now both feet are inside, fully on board, ready to kick some ass.

...........................................................

**If you've made a backup plan, you haven't made a decision.**

...........................................................

The Latin roots of the word "decide" literally mean "to cut off," meaning all other options fall away and you are committed to the decision alone. People have such meltdowns and resistance around making decisions, because they panic and fear that by deciding on one thing, they will miss out on all the other cool things they want to do. Meanwhile:

........................................................

You can't do anything if you try to do everything.

........................................................

One of the biggest banana peels on the road to success is fragmenting your time and focus. If you're all over the place, you're half-assing a bunch of different things instead of kicking ass at one thing. Figure out how you're going to get rich, make the no-nonsense decision to keep going until you reach your goal, and, as part of your reward, you'll get to do all the other things you couldn't do while you were busy sticking by your decision to get rich.

If you ripped this page out of this book and did just this one thing—decided with 100 percent commitment that you will get rich and stick to your resolve to do so until you're rollin' in it—you would be victorious. Because when you decide, you automatically become obsessed with thoughts of making it happen, you're looking everywhere for opportunities, scary ones, your faith is strong like bull because if you didn't believe getting rich was possible you wouldn't have decided to do it in the first place, you're grateful that what you desire already exists, it's all you think about and has become real in your mind, you take huge risks, and you have zero patience for anyone who tells you it's not going to work. Think about it—you can make a decision as menial as changing the color of your bathroom and you're suddenly a force of nature, looking at the paint on walls you've seen a million times a whole new way, talking excitedly about nothing else, inspiring friends to leap behind plants when they see you approaching with yet more paint samples in your hands. A firm decision sets everything in motion—your mindset and your actions—and also alerts Universal Intelligence that this is how it's going to be, and it starts moving everything you need in your direction.

..................................................................

Your desires are brought to you via thought, and you receive them by deciding to take action.

..................................................................

I want to point out here that when I say that the Universe starts moving everything you need in your direction, this goes for ideas as well as opportunities, people, and things. When you make a decision and alert Universal Intelligence to bring it on, you have to pay close attention to any thoughts and big new ideas that come into your head. You must catch yourself before your old conditioning can fling itself in your path and try to block the new you. *What, just jump on a plane and show up on Uncle Steve's doorstep to ask him for a job? No way! That's insane!* One good idea that comes in out of nowhere can change your entire life, but it ain't gonna do nothing if you don't act on it, and your subconscious is so ninja it can stop you without you even realizing what's happening.

..............................................................................................

Brilliant ideas are love notes from the Universe that
say: *This is for you. I think you're hot. And capable.
Go share your stunning youness with the world.*

..............................................................................................

I can't tell you how much time I wasted (okay, forty years)
pretending I could do things differently, instead of acting on
ideas that seemed out of my reach or would have cost me
money I didn't want to spend. In other words, ideas that would
have forced me to grow. I blazed by countless strokes of genius
without even giving these ideas the time of day, just instantly
tossed them aside as impossible. Next! Then back to complaining, spinning out, wondering why oh why can't I get out of my
suckhole? The Universe must have been like, *I just gave you
exactly what you asked for! Are you freaking kidding me?*

A great example of a life-changing idea is one that came
to our poor climber stranded on the mountain. One of the
few possessions that somehow made it through his ordeal was
his wristwatch. As he's lying in the blinding snow gazing
across the insane amount of ground he has to cover with his
janky leg and empty water bottle, he picks a spot off in the
distance where there's a bit of an incline or a drop off or
something noticeable that marks it, and decides he has to get
there in twenty minutes. He sets the timer on his watch and
no matter how much pain he's in or what obstacles he happens upon along the way, all his thoughts, energy, and determination are focused on getting to that spot before the timer

goes off. He said it was the only way he could handle crossing the devastating expanse before him without completely flipping out about how impossible it seemed. He took each twenty-minute challenge extremely seriously. He made reaching his goal before the timer went off nonnegotiable and urgent, and understood that if he blew it, a whole lot more was at stake than just losing against a wristwatch.

When we set out to make big changes in our lives, it's very common for the beast of overwhelm to lunge. We still have everything going on in our present lives, and now we're adding more stuff to our to-do list in order to achieve new goals? Are you kidding me? And it's not just more stuff, it's all the big scary stuff that we've been too wimpy to do up until now and it's all so big and crazy and suddenly you feel like, *Holy crap, I can't move. Seriously, I think something happened to my arms, I can't lift them. . . .* And then, once again, mastering your mindset comes to the rescue. Overwhelm, just like calm, is a state of mind, and all you have to do is choose which party you're going to attend.

........................................................................

Overwhelm: When you make the unhelpful decision
to stop breathing, lose perspective, and forget
you're in control of your life.

........................................................................

Here are a couple of ways to beat the beast of overwhelm back into its cage:

1. Investigate the specifics. We cause ourselves so much unnecessary pain when we fly off the handle and assume that the vague, infinite details of our lives are crushing us to death. Meanwhile, we usually have no idea what we're talking about. For example: *I have a million e-mails to answer and I have to pick up the kids and make dinner and I have to apply for a loan for my new business—I am never going to get it all done!* becomes, post investigation: *The e-mails will take forty-five minutes to answer because there are actually twelve of them, not a million, dinner takes thirty minutes to throw together, I can get my neighbor to pick up the kids, and I'll have plenty of time to fill out my loan application. Oh.* Certainly there are some times when we've bitten off more than we can chew, but I promise you, the majority of your overwhelm can be set at ease by getting some clarity.

2. Chunk your to-dos down into bite-sized pieces. Facing the task of writing an entire book will make you want to lie down in the road; sitting down to write one chapter is exciting. Facing the task of doubling your income by studying your ass off, getting into medical school, going to medical school, interning, and opening a private practice will make you envy your bartender's career choice; digging into the information in the first chapter of your medical textbook is exciting. Facing the task of traversing miles and miles of unfriendly, frozen terrain with a body that's been through a wood chipper will make you want to exit stage right; spending the next twenty minutes getting from point A to point B

with the same wood-chipped body is not exciting but, you know, sucks less.

The other critical thing chunking your time does is provide focus. Using the example of the dude stuck on the mountain again, during his twenty-minute spurts he was focused on nothing but the task at hand. This focus did two things: One, it strengthened his faith. What you focus on you create more of, and all he focused on was hauling his ass to the desired endpoint. End of story. No thoughts of stopping or failing or boohooing. He focused solely on the possibility of success and that's what he achieved over and over, and each time he did, his faith got stronger. Second, this steadfast focus helped him maximize his time. The dude did not have the luxury of screwing around, writing his name with his pee in a snowbank, or making snow angels, he was in serious need of a glass of water pronto, so every second counted.

We too are going to die, and every second counts in our lives, but we tend to forget about this urgency and spend our precious time on Earth procrastinating, whining, focusing on and believing in thoughts that hold us back instead of getting the job done. People who spend eight hours a day at a job spend about three collective hours being productive and the rest of the time hanging out at the water cooler, staring blankly into the fridge in the break room, thinking about sex, watching ducks chase a dog around a bush on Facebook, etc. If you feel like you have all the time in the world to do something, you will take all the time in the world. If you have twenty minutes, the task will take you twenty minutes. Chunking down your time and demanding that you focus on one thing and one thing only creates urgency, maximizes your productivity, and frees up more time for you to do other things.

......................................................................

Time comes to those who make it, not those who try to find it.

......................................................................

Here's a breakdown of the action steps we've gone over so far that will help you put a new bulge in your wallet:

- Get clear on the amount of money you're going to make, the specifics of what the money's for, and how freaking awesome it feels to make it.

- Decide, with unshakable commitment, that you are making this money.

- Get a plan together to make the money you desire to make, chunk the plan back into bite-sized pieces, and focus yer ass off on one goal at a time.

- Hold an image in your mind of the life you're creating and all the money that's flowing toward you with eager excitement, hardcore faith, and deep gratitude.

- Do your best wherever you're at. If, while building your greeting card empire, you've taken a job scraping gum off the bottom of tables at a bowling alley, instead of being pissed off about having a job that you don't exactly love (what you focus on you create more of), find the silver lining, be the best damn gum scraper that table has ever worked with, and have an attitude of gratitude.

.........................................................................

A desire to grow is not the same as being negative
about where you're at.

.........................................................................

- When the Universe presents a How that leads in the direction of your goal to make more money, instead of talking yourself out of it, leap into its lovin' arms immediately. Especially if it's scary. When the thoughts come to you, all you need to answer for yourself are these three questions: Is this something I want to be, do, or have? Is this leading me in the direction of my goal? Is it going to screw anybody over if I do this? If you get satisfactory answers to those questions, go for it.

.........................................................................

Let your fear be your compass.

.........................................................................

Remember that $85,000 I told you I manifested to pay for my big fat coaching package? Well I'ma tell you how I did it because it was right up there with one of the scariest, most uncomfortable things I've ever done. Once I decided to get coached at that level for reals, instead of running and hiding like I did the first time around, I acted on an idea that came into my mind the moment it arrived. This idea was not something that was fun or comfortable or anything I'd pass up having a full-body waxing session to go do, but I did it because my desire to kick ass was stronger than my desire to waste more time living the life I was living. I got the idea of someone I could maybe borrow that money from, someone who a) knew very little about coaching, and what she did know probably brought to mind words like "snake oil" and "manipulative garbage" and "bunch of weirdos"; b) is the most Frugal McDugal person I'd ever met, the kind who has money but never, ever spends it except to stockpile toilet paper when it goes on sale; c) believed in me.

I bought a plane ticket to fly to her house the moment the terrifying thought took over my brain (which cost about a thousand dollars more than usual thanks to the last minuteness of it all) and arrived on her doorstep, surprising the hell out of her. I risked being vulnerable to this person, I risked her thinking I was out of my mind, irresponsible, very possibly in a cult. And I will never forget the pained face she made when I told her how much I needed. But after much uncomfortable discussion, she forked it over. And I proceeded not only to make the money to pay her back in less than a year, but thanks to the fact that I'd faced my terror and asked, along with getting a year of some of the best coaching I ever got, I went where no Jen Sincero had ever gone before. I took huge, terrifying risks on a consistent basis, hired a team to create videos and improve my online structures unlike the old days of doing it all myself, created new products and services, upped my rates and reached out to clients who were "out of my league," sat my ass down and wrote a book that became a *New York Times* bestseller—basically I did all the things I was too scared/cheap/lazy to do before, and all of which led to the seven-figure business and brand I have today. And it never would have happened if I hadn't started by doing something I sooooooooooooooo did not want to do.

IMPORTANT $85,000 NOTE: If you're reading this and thinking, *Oh yeah, I'll just scoot on out and ask all the many people I know with $85,000 lying around for a loaner,* I want to be clear. The price tag is irrelevant; transforming your life is about your desire and your decision, it's not about what solutions may or may not be right in front of you. If you decide you absolutely must manifest a certain amount of money to provide yourself with the resources to get rich, be it $80 or $80,000, the money exists, it's just a matter of how serious you are about getting it for yourself. One of the fastest ways of talking yourself out of doing what you need to do to succeed is collapsing into victimhood, deciding that other people have more available to them, and that you have it harder, so why bother. You very well may have it harder than most people, but people who've had it even harder than you have done miraculous things with their lives. Success is not about where you're at, it's about where, and who, you decide you're going to be.

When you decide to get rich, the options are out there, and while they might take awhile for you to wake up to, when you do, it will all come down to how badly you want change.

### SUCCESS STORY: IF SHE CAN DO IT, SO CAN YOU.

*A client of mine, Kelly, went from making an average of $4,500 a month to an average of $35,000 a month by scaring the crap out of herself.*

*Kelly has her own T-shirt company. At the time, she was frustrated by the fact that no matter how much money she made, she always barely had enough to get by. Something always came up that sucked it away— her car would break down, an unexpected bill would show up, a family member would need bail money. She wanted to take on more business, but couldn't handle more on her own and she felt she was too busy to train someone. Then, when business was slow, she told herself she couldn't afford to hire and train some- one because business was slow. She stayed in this loop for years and years:*

I had convinced myself that there was no way I could hire someone. I was late on my mortgage, didn't have any new business coming in, and I kept thinking, *how can I be responsible for someone else's income too?*

When my coach told me I had to commit to hiring someone if I wanted to grow, I was utterly terrified. But then my mindset suddenly shifted—it was like, once I was given permission to do it, I had this epiphany that, of course, it's so obvious this is what I have to do. Before this shift there was no way I could see it.

The second I committed to making the hire, I had no choice, I had to make the money to pay him. It totally terrified me, but also totally motivated me. I knew immediately I'd made the right decision because once he started working for me, the floodgates opened and all the business I was psychically pushing away started coming toward me. There was no way I could have handled all the business that came in without him.

After our first coaching session, I raised my frequency by making the scary but exciting commitment to bring someone else on, visualized and said affirmations about bringing in the money I desired to make, and within the first week wound up making $26,000. In one week! I feel like it was 50 percent magic, 50 percent hard work.

What a wonderful feeling to not wake up in the middle of the night stressing out about money!

Human beings have unlimited potential and most of us are just scraping the surface of our powers. If you're not where you want to be financially, think about where you're holding back. We pretend we've done everything we can and we work harder and harder doing the same things we've always done, hoping for different results. Meanwhile, there is almost always a solution right in front of our faces that we're ignoring because we've decided it's out of the question.

# THERE'S A BIG DIFFERENCE BETWEEN CAN'T AND DON'T WANNA

Getting rich is not necessarily about working harder. In fact, it is usually about working less, because you're making smarter choices. When Kelly hired her first employee, she no longer had to work as hard as she was working AND she massively increased her income. So much so that she purchased two, count 'em, two new printing machines, hired a second employee, and started looking for a bigger space for her business. All within a few months. And it all started because she made the decision to grow and did the one thing that scared the living crap out of her that she knew would get her to her goal.

## LAST RESORT SPENDING

Sometimes the scary risk we need to take to get to the next level is spending money we don't yet have. It's the money version of leap and the net will appear, and it's a very controversial topic, because basically what I'm saying is go into debt, and debt is the big bad wolf in our society. But debt, like everything else, is all about your mindset. Spending money you don't have recklessly, living beyond your means, digging a deep old hole for yourself with a mindset of fear and denial and no real drive or plan to pay it off is one mindset. I am not recommending you do this. I am also not recommending you go into debt if you feel there are other options—this is a last resort option but a viable one *only if you've got the right mindset in place*. Going out on a limb and demanding of yourself that you rise to the occasion and do not stop until you make the money back is the mindset I'm talking about. It's like when you want to go on a trip but you can never find the right time. Buy the damn ticket, book the hotels, get everything in place, and then work your schedule to fit around it. If you wait for time to open up, it will never happen.

Same with this—if you wait to have the money first, it may never happen. I did this over and over when I was stretching myself to get out of my rickety-ass lifestyle and become rich. I got new credit cards to pay for my coaching, and then did everything my coaches told me to do, no matter how terrifying, to make the money back, and each time I paid my debts off within months. If I had waited until I made the money I needed at my then income of thirty grand a year, I never would have been able to hire a coach and feed myself at the same time. I had to take the terrifying leap of going deeper into debt, but I did it with total faith in myself, because I was ready to turn my life around. Taking these types of risks is about being in charge of your life rather than a victim. It's about having faith in the Universe, and yourself, that you can and will manifest anything you desire. It's about who you become in this process.

If you need to take out a loan to rent a space to put your new store in or borrow money to pay your new assistant, put a plan in place to pay off your debts and demand of yourself that you make the money back. You don't get anywhere sitting around inside your comfort zone. Receive and spend the money with faith and gratitude that it's coming back to you, keep your frequency high and your focus strong, demand of yourself that you do everything, especially taking many more scary leaps to new heights, to make the money back, and do not stop until you do.

## TO GET RICH

Suggested Money Mantra (say it, write it, feel it, own it):
*I love money because I am a fearless, badass, moneymaking machine.*

1. Anticipate your obstacles. Doubt is like the little string you tug on that unravels the whole sweater. Get clear on the top three things that could bring doubt to your resolve and prepare yourself to meet them head-on so they are powerless over you. (Example: *My spouse won't be supportive of me.* Have a mantra ready: *Only I know my own truth and I know in my bones that I am rich.* Write down the obstacles and write down the solutions.)

2. Raise your bottom line. So often our decision muscle only really kicks in when our backs are against the wall and we have to make the money—rent is due, we need surgery, the Mafia is at the door with an IOU. Decide on an amount that is going to be your new bottom line so it's no longer zero. Let's say five hundred dollars. You have to have five hundred dollars in your bank account at all times, and the second you get near that amount, you sound the rallying cry to up your

game and bring in more money so you don't go below that amount. Then keep raising your bottom line every month or so and soon you'll no longer be in a struggle.

3. Spend money in new ways. Buy something extravagant to raise your frequency and remind yourself that you are in the flow and that money is a renewable resource. Something expensive, exciting, something that won't break the bank but that feels decadent, has great meaning to you, and inspires you to kick some ass.

4. Make one big, hairy, scary nonnegotiable decision right now that will move you toward your financial goal and do it. I mean it, right now. Something you've had in the back of your mind that you know would totally change your world but have been too scared to do. Snooze not, lose not. There's no time like the present.

Please fill in the blank:

I'm grateful to money because _____.

# CHAPTER 9

# MOVIN' ON UP

When I was in my early twenties, I moved to Barcelona, Spain, with a bunch of friends from college. We rented a run-down apartment in a shady part of town, dragged all of our furniture in off the street, drank like fiends, lived like pigs, rocked and rolled all night, and partied every day.

Because Spain is right around the corner from Italy, I decided one weekend to take the train to Naples and visit my relatives on my dad's side of the family. I couldn't wait to party in the old country with my cousin Valentina, check out the local scene, get to know her better, and present her with the giant chunk of hash I had hidden inside a box of tampons for her.

When I arrived, I discovered, much to my horror, that our big Saturday night out involved gathering a bunch of her friends together and strolling around the plaza, eating gelatos and people watching. If we were feeling especially wild, we'd go back and get another gelato. It was like going into rehab. As disappointed as I was, I couldn't help feeling a pang of shame every time we passed a bunch of staggering American twentysomethings, drunkenly shouting "Oh solo mio!" in the streets.

Unlike American me, Valentina grew up with a bottle of wine on her dinner table, and was not met with a raised parental eyebrow and a *Just what the hell do you think you're doing?* should her underaged hand reach for it. This is partly why she was having wholesome, Annette Funicello evenings out, and why I was on my way to waking up in the emergency room with a stomach-pumping tube shoved down my throat. And returning home with my hash untouched.

To her, booze was no big deal, it was part of everyday life. A bottle of wine had the same excitement factor as the loaf of bread next to it on the table. To me, however, it was taboo, dangerous, as thrilling and irreverent as smoking cigarettes or calling people's parents by their first names. I was over twenty-one, nobody was the boss of me anymore, I could do whatever I wanted, and so I did, no matter how nauseated it made me.

Our environment shapes everything from our drinking habits to our financial situations to our physical appearance, and the longer we immerse ourselves in certain surroundings, the more they influence us. Ever notice how people start to look like their dogs after a while? Or how you start to say tomahto instead of tomato the longer you hang out in England? And I don't know about you, but I have a closetful of stuff I bought on vacation—a twenty-five-pound knitted woolen sweater from Iceland, rings for all my toes from India, a pointy straw hat that makes me look like a drink umbrella from Vietnam, all of which I wore constantly while away, none of which have yet to leave my closet now that I'm home.

When it comes to money, who and what you surround yourself with has a huge effect on how you perceive it and feel about it. Your environment helps define what you consider to be expensive or cheap, a wise or stupid purchase, and how much you'll allow yourself to make. In fact, here's a sobering exercise: Take the average income of the five people you hang around with most, and you'll most likely find yours.

Had I stayed in Italy and hung out with Valentina, I probably would have avoided the bloated twenty pounds of alcohol weight I gained in Barcelona and I'd still have the bracelet my grandmother gave me that I lost wagering on a drunken game of darts one night (I suck at darts, what was I thinking?). At that time in my life, however, I ran with a boozy tribe, I prided myself on my unbroken record of downing a beer bong in under ten seconds, I wasn't interested in the finer things in life like good health and waking up in places I remembered walking into.

Without giving it much thought, we accept our environment to be "reality," to represent what normal life looks like—doesn't everyone know how to do a keg stand? This is why, when you decide to upgrade your income and standard of living, it's important to put yourself in the new environment you're intent on creating for yourself as best you can: It not only jars you out of your old way of thinking, believing, and being, but it gives the new environment an opportunity to start having an effect on you and to start becoming your new idea of normal instead of *As if! Me?*

Go test-drive the car you'd love to buy, every week. Walk around in the stores you can't wait to shop in and try on clothes. Stroll through the neighborhoods you'll buy a house in one day and pick out the one you like best. Hang out in the international terminal of the airport, go to the marina and check out the boats, watch documentaries about people rafting down the Grand Canyon, show up on the free days at the gym you're going to join—whatever it is that turns you on, go soak in it.

Back in my money-free days, I was living in Los Angeles way over on the east side in a neighborhood I didn't like but could afford. I braved crosstown traffic several times a week to go hang out in a neighborhood all the way on the west side, by the beach, that I really wanted to live in but felt was too expensive. I loved the idea of living by the ocean, hearing the waves crashing while I drifted off to sleep, taking long walks as the sun set over the water, waiting in line at the bank alongside guys in wet suits holding surfboards under their arms. That's how I wanted to roll. Only problem was, that's the way a lot of people wanted to roll, and finding a place to live at the beach cost basically twice what I was paying at the time in the neighborhood I hated. Or at least that's what everyone said, including Craigslist.

I made the thirty-five-minute drive to the beach nearly every other day anyway, set myself up at a coffee shop in the neighborhood I wanted to live in, and pretended I'd just walked there from my place. I told everyone who stood still long enough that I was looking for an apartment, hung up flyers, read the obituaries, told all my friends and asked them to tell their friends—I did everything but put on a sandwich board and hand out my phone number to people on the sidewalk. For months, I couldn't find anything anywhere near my price range, and then one day something came up on Craigslist that was three blocks from the beach and only a hundred bucks more than what I was already paying. It sounded too good to be true, and when I went to the open house, it was packed, because apparently everyone else thought it was too good to be true too. But the ad didn't lie: It was three blocks from the beach, crazy cheap for that part of town, and it was "cozy." What the ad didn't say is that its last tenant was a Toyota Corolla, because the apartment used to be a garage. A one-car garage, let us be clear. But I wanted to live by the beach and this place was my ticket in, so I wrote a love note about the apartment on my application, called the landlord and told him how serious and tidy I was, showed up the next day while he was painting the place and brought him a pastrami sandwich on rye, and finally, probably just to get me to leave him alone, he rented it to me.

I realize that me moving into my dream one-car garage isn't all that compelling a financial success story, but the reason I'm sharing it is because it was a stepping-stone. It put me in the environment that I dearly desired to be in, and it was from that cheerful little crap heap that I took my first big steps toward making real money, which resulted in me moving out of the garage and into a real live house soon thereafter. But while I was garaging it, I fancied the place up the best I could, painted the bars on the windows a nice bright white, made mobiles out of shells and rocks and hung them from the ventilation pipes on the ceiling, and covered the cracks in the warped garage doors with frames purchased at the dollar store and filled them with photos of my friends. The fact that I could smell and hear the ocean, that I could ride my bike everywhere and swim whenever I felt like it made a gigantic difference in my energy and my outlook on life. I felt inspired, happy and in my element, and I had also proven to everyone, including myself, that I could do the impossible—I found an apartment in Venice Beach that was cheap.

We are energetic beings driven by emotion, so if your surroundings depress you, it's critical that you do whatever you can to brighten things up. Slap on a fresh coat of paint, clean your windows, hang up pictures from magazines of places you'd love to live in or visit and look at them all the time, get some plants, tidy up your clutter, throw a nice bedspread over your ratty couch, and if you've got sheets thumbtacked over the windows, please, get some damn curtains. I have some friends who are getting ready to sell their house so they cleaned the crap out of it, painted the rusty back door, weeded the yard, patched all the holes in the walls, did all these things to fancy it up to sell and were mortified that they didn't bother to do it while they lived there because it completely changed the feel of the place.

You don't need to spend loads of money or time on this— little things can make a huge difference—and this is much more than an adventure in Martha Stewart Land. This is an investment in your potential. Beauty can grow from the muck, but not without the proper nourishment and energy.

Shabby is as shabby does, so take one day, one little day, and spend it tending to raising the frequency of your surroundings.

This goes for everything in your physical environment. The clothes you wear, the food you eat, the music you listen to, the places you stroll—be very conscious of what brings you joy, purposefully participate in those things as best you can, and ditch anything that brings you down or makes you yawn.

My friend told me this hilarious story about having a French roommate who was watching her get changed one day and said, in her thick Parisian accent, "Your underwear makes me believe you are sad and hate your life." My friend looked down at her utilitarian cotton panties, an old pair from a five-pack purchased at Target and thought, *But they're bikinis, at least they're not the high-waisted granny ones, doesn't that count for something?*

The most important part of your environment to be conscious of is the people you surround yourself with. Especially when you're just starting to flex your new faith muscles, plow past all your doubt, fears, and worries, and get some real money flowing into your life. You need all the strength you've got, and there ain't no bigger oil slick than the peer, friend, or family member who lobs an unhelpful zinger in your path like, "I just read an article about how four out of five new restaurants don't make it. You could lose everything you've got if your restaurant idea fails."

.............................................................

Nothing pops our balloon of belief like the pointy
pin of a pal.

.............................................................

Make an effort to surround yourself with people who cheer you on and offer support, not who hand you a "Good luck with that!" bag of turds, or the ole favorite, "I'm telling you these (negative) things because I'm worried about you, I'm just trying to help." That's basically them saying, "I'm small and scared and I'm rubbing it all over you, but you can't object because it means I care." Worriers, doubters, freakers, sad sacks, small thinkers, complainers, naysayers, whiners, chunters, grumpers, scaredy cats—these are not the people you want to share your dreams with.

The problem is, upgrading your environment in the human department is a bit more challenging than putting down some throw rugs or planting sunflowers in your yard, especially if the most unhelpful people happen to be related to you. This is one of the most common, and upsetting, conundrums people go through when they decide to get rich, so you are not alone if you're wondering WTF.

Here's what you can do when your peeps are negative, fearful, and don't support your ass kickery:

- Do not try to change them. Encourage them, love them, offer advice when asked, tell them you think they're the bee's knees, but don't make it your project to try to get them to see the light. First of all, you can't get them to do anything unless they're willing to evolve. If they're stuck in fear about you changing your life, as well as fearful about changing their own lives, they will wake up if and when they're ready to, not when you tell them to. Second of all, it's their journey, their choice on how they ride it out. Third of all, it will put everyone involved in a bad mood because you'll feel frustrated and they'll feel nagged.

- Lead by example. Instead of telling them what they should and shouldn't be doing, work on yourself, become the best you can be, and if they ask how you did it, do all you can to help them, and if they don't ask, leave them alone.

- Do not share your dreams with them or the work you're doing on yourself if they've proven to you that they're not going to support you and/or will fling their doubt and worry in your face. What's the point? You still get to love them and be with them, you just don't involve them in that part of your life.

- Hang out with people who are going places, who understand and support the path you're on, who are your new tribe. If you don't know any people like this, find some. Figure it out. Go to coaching seminars, find people on social media, take classes, start a self-help book group—if you're serious about it you will find your people.

When the people in our lives who we love aren't supportive of the journey we're on it's excruciating because, hello, what's more important than the people in our lives who we love? Our connection to them is one of the most vital things we've got, and when we start to grow and change and they don't come with us, a big ole can of worms often gets unearthed for everyone involved. It unleashes the Great Human Fear at the Bottom of All Other Fears: *I will be abandoned* (by people, by all that's familiar, by my identity, by my life = I'll die, etc.). And the reality is, if we're going to fully blossom into who we truly are, we have to be willing to let these relationships go.

IMPORTANT LETTING GO NOTE: Being willing to let people go does not mean that they will definitely go. But you can't cling to the old you and your old relationships and grow into the new you at the same time. You have to choose one or the other: Cling and stay or grow and release and see if they come along for the ride.

I see it go both ways all the time. I've seen plenty of marriages break up when one person is moving forward and the other is stuck in fear, and I've seen people come closer together than they ever imagined they could because they both opened up to who they were becoming (sometimes it takes awhile for the other person to come around, but not always). You don't know what is going to happen, you have no guarantee that someone in your life will freak out or laugh at you or have an epiphany and come join you on your joy ride to awesomeness. Trying to troubleshoot outcomes, denying yourself your dreams, not daring to take large leaps so the people around you won't be all "someone's gotten mighty big for her britches!" is a complete waste of time (and your life). Focus on you, and what makes you hop back and forth from foot to foot in excitement, because not living your life is no way to live.

................................................................

When you succumb to fear, you are under the illusion
that you can predict the future.

................................................................

We waste so much time letting our fears push us around and half the time our fears and doubts never even freaking pan out! You'd think we would have caught on to that one by now. Stay focused on your desires, not your fears, and trust that everything will fall into place as it's meant to. What happens as you grow and change is you peel away the layers of your old self, and things of a lower nature drop away in order to make room for things of a higher nature. These could be parts of your old identity, it could be that old-ass bathrobe you refuse to throw away that you've had since college, it could be relationships that no longer serve you or the other person ("lower nature" here means people/things you've outgrown, that are not aligned with who you're becoming, btw, it doesn't mean that you're suddenly above or better than anyone/anything). Whatever it is you're shedding, you must surrender the low to make space for the high if you're going to grow.

Here are some key ways hanging with high-frequency people will help you get rich.

## THEY BOOST YOUR ENERGY

Think about how you feel after you hear a particularly inspiring speaker give a talk, or hang out with a friend who's on fire with his business and who bats brilliant ideas back and forth with you over beers on his deck or when you're just generally having a blast doing what you love with awesome people—it's like you could bench-press a Buick you're so pumped up. And think about how you feel when you're around people who complain about what a dick their boss is or how impossible it is to find a good babysitter or how screwed we all are because Social Security will be gone by the time we need it. It's like they just emptied a hamper full of wet socks onto your lap. We are energetic creatures, and when you've made the commitment to change your life and to get rich, one of the most important things you can do is be militant about the types of energy you subject yourself to. Surround yourself with people whose energy lights you up and it will empower you to get rich.

## THEY STRENGTHEN YOUR FAITH

Being around confident, wealth-positive people whom you respect gives you permission to believe there is abundance available to you too. No matter how impossible a situation may seem, a superconfident person who believes in something without a doubt is a force of nature that can inspire you to reach great heights.

I used to go backpacking with these friends of mine who would take me out into the middle of nowhere in the wilderness areas of southeast Utah on a regular basis. How they knew where the hell they were going and how to get us back was an utter mystery to me. We'd set off through a canyon, walk out onto a huge expanse of sand, climb over endless boulders, hike up a river, pick our way through a wash, and then five days later, boink, we'd pop out right where the car was parked.

On one of these trips we hired a lady who ran a jeep operation to drop us off at the mouth of some canyon. When we met her at her garage she told us there was a big hatching of rattlesnakes in the very canyon we were going into, and that the place was crawling with them. My friends are listening to her, completely unfazed, as they load their things into the jeep. I'm squirming as if I'm watching a horror movie and the soon-to-be victim doesn't realize that the call is coming from inside the house. *She said rattlesnakes! Hatched! Lots of them! In our canyon!* This woman knew some shit, she was as craggy and leathery as the canyon walls themselves, but my friends just let her finish her little snake story, as if having to endure her describe the cute thing her dog did that morning, before asking her if there was any water to be had down there or would we have to carry our own in?

I totally trusted my friends and had complete faith in them, so if they weren't scared of spending their last moments on Earth with rattlesnake venom pulsing through their veins, I wasn't scared. And off my faith and I leapt into the canyon behind them, emerging six days later with nary a bite nor a rattlesnake sighting.

··········································································

Faith is contagious.

··········································································

Surround yourself with people who have unwavering faith in themselves, in you, and in our abundant Universe and it will help you take the giant leaps you need to take to get yerself rich.

## THEY UP YOUR GAME

If you're around people who are making money in great and joyful ways, you'll not only see what's possible for you, but you'll be motivated to push yourself. If you're around people who are ripping bongloads on the couch all day, you'll feel like a hero for getting your laundry done.

Healthy competition is a wonderful thing. Surround yourself with people who are bringing their A game and you will want to bring your A game too.

## THEY MAKE YOU MIGHTIER

There's a great story about an army that's about to cross a bridge, and the captain tells his soldiers to walk out of step with one another because if they're all in sync, the momentum will make the bridge do that crazy bendy thing that bridges do right before they snap. People in motion moving together in a group create a massive force strong enough to rip a bridge in half. Coming together with kick-ass people and sharing your resources, your ideas, your connections, your know-how, your enthusiasm, and your snacks can take you all much further and way faster than if you were working on your own. Surround yourself with generous, creative, big thinkers and you'll maximize your opportunities to get rich.

## THEY CELEBRATE WHO YOU ARE

Everyone talks about how you know who your true friends are when you're desperate and things really bottom out. But I want to send a shout-out to the friends who stick by you when you're kicking ass. When you're stuck in the suckhole and people come to your rescue, they get the opportunity to feel helpful, to save the day, to be a hero. Don't get me wrong, it's a beautiful, essential thing to take care of one another, and I'm hugely grateful to everyone who's ever helped me when I was in the dumps, but I think more needs to be said about the friends who selflessly cheer you on when you're totally killing it. Especially if they're not doing so great themselves. Your success forces them to look at their life and think about what they could do differently, which usually makes people fairly grouchy. Surround yourself with people who have your back and celebrate your successes no matter what.

> **SUCCESS STORY: IF SHE CAN DO IT, SO CAN YOU.**
>
> *Jill, 42, went from making an average of $2,500 a month to an average of $45,000 a month:*
>     While I was #1 in recruiting for my direct sales company, I was making only $2,000 to $3,000 per month.

I decided to start coaching direct sellers on social media strategy, and now make an average of $40,000 to $50,000 per month, with growth goals to double that next year.

In direct sales/networking marketing, it is very easy to believe in a hoarder mentality—meaning, "I better hoard my knowledge/information/contacts, because if I share it, someone will compete against me." I teach abundance mentality. This is 100 percent about believing that there is enough business for all, and that the Universe will reward you for putting good out there. I have dozens and dozens of examples of clients who have manifested business to them, based on a positive and abundance-oriented mindset—even when there are thousands of other sellers selling the same products online.

I didn't have any major fears about money. My challenges were more tactical in nature. I had ideas of how I wanted the outcome to look, but I didn't know what tools or systems I needed. I invested in a business coach and hired support staff before I was making enough money to justify it. I wanted to have the systems in place to be able to scale quickly—which I have. I am now at the point where I will be raising my rates again at year-end, because I've created offerings to support the lower end of my market.

I have a very tight group of friends, and they are my cheerleaders, accountability partners, and sounding board. I also meditate, read, and have been known to cry when I'm scared. Then I try to think, *Is this the role model I want to be for my clients?* I teach a BRAVE philosophy. In direct sales, you are competing against many others who sell the same products or services. So what will make you stand out? Being BRAVE and different—online, in person, with confidence and poise. Practice twenty seconds of insane bravery and amazing things will happen. Find a business coach and make the investment. Follow their advice to the letter, change your systems, get out of your own way, and do it.

My husband and I live by the belief that money doesn't make you happy, money gives you options. So we've been able to pay off debt, travel, invest in our savings and retirement. But I don't believe money has changed us.

## TO GET RICH

Suggested Money Mantra (say it, write it, feel it, own it): *I love money because it makes me more of who I truly am.*

1. Make a vision board. Cut out pictures of places, things, experiences, types of people you are excited to experience in your new, richer life and hang it somewhere where you'll see it often.

2. Make a list of all the things you might have to give up on your road to riches. Think of people, items, old identities, etc.—if they don't bring you joy and inspiration, either get

rid of them or pull back from them (instead of fighting to keep them). With the people in your life, start slowly and release them gently. Maybe it's about not sharing your dreams and victories with them if they can't handle it, or maybe it's about letting go of the need to make them see things your way and trying to change them, or maybe it's about hanging out with them less. Notice the specifics of what's not working between you and them, and make some changes. This will give everyone room to be whoever they need to be in the face of your transformation, as well as free up room for high-frequency people and things to come into your life.

3. Improve your environment. Pay attention to how the things you surround yourself with make you feel. Pick at least one thing in all the following areas and upgrade in a way that gives you even more joy and energy:

- Your home

- Your car

- Your clothes

- Your general appearance

- Your exercise routine

- The food you eat

- The music you listen to

- The news you pay attention to

4. Make two new high-vibe friends. Get clear on the specifics of what they're like and how they make you feel and write these things down. Then, using the suggestions in this chapter, make a conscious effort to find high-frequency, wealth-conscious people to surround yourself with. Have faith and gratitude that they exist, do everything you can think of to find them, and know that they are out there looking for you too.

5. Start a mastermind group with one or two people. Meet over the phone once a week, give each person a specific amount of time to brainstorm and focus on their goals for getting rich (fifteen or thirty minutes usually) before moving on to the other person. Do this only with high-vibe, ass-kicking people!

Please fill in the blank:

I'm grateful to money because _____.

## CHAPTER 10

# AND NOW, A WORD FROM MY ACCOUNTANT . . .

I was very fortunate to grow up in a safe, suburban neighborhood with lots of room to roam and a tribe of kids more or less my own age. We'd make forts by the river, build nests in trees, sled down Mrs. Randall's huge hill, catch fireflies in jars, play kick the can, lock my little sister and her friends in the closet and issue them their orders: 1) Bring us each two peanut butter and jelly sandwiches, no crust, twice as much jelly as peanut butter. 2) Take off your underpants, wear them on your head. 3) Make a phony phone call to the pizza parlor and order Mrs. Malloch (the old lady across the street) two sausage calzones. You have ten minutes. For each minute you go over you will have to eat one dog biscuit. GO! THE TIMER IS TICKING!

Our house was often the center of action for a few reasons, the top three being: We had a ping-pong table, my mom bought Twinkies, and the burn book. The burn book was one of many in a stack of medical books my dad kept in his den, and it contained the most gruesome pictures of human bodily misfortune you could imagine. Big, glossy, well-lit shots of people in the hospital with half their faces melted, giant oozy pustules on their arms, a foot charred black as a burnt marshmallow. We'd huddle around, and whoever won the coin toss would get to open it and either flip through the pages or make everyone stare at one particularly grisly shot. We never made it more than a minute or so before the book was slammed shut and we'd tear through the house, screaming our heads off.

I was too proud to admit it, but I hated the burn book. I got scared looking at those pictures, imagining how much pain those people were in. More than once I had a nightmare where I looked in the mirror and saw my own face melted off. But it was mostly the pain that I couldn't bear to witness and, to this day, I still become paralyzed when faced with even the wimpiest injury, mine or someone else's. My most recent mishap, which involved having the entire toenail on my big toe ripped off—the details of which I'm not going into because it wasn't pretty and was pretty bloody—got blown totally out of proportion. The doctor cleaned the toe and wrapped it in miles of gauze and tape and I walked around with what looked like a gong mallet sticking off the front of my foot for weeks. If I were a rational adult, I would have removed the gauze two or three days later and replaced it with some ointment and a simple Band-Aid, but I chose to keep limping, showering with a plastic baggie over my foot, and favoring open-toed footwear for as long as I possibly could so I wouldn't have to take off the filthy gauze mound and face what was underneath.

This is how so many broke people act when it comes to money. We'd rather limp around taped to our ratty, unhealthy relationships with money, afraid that if we peel back the layers, we won't be able to handle what we see underneath. But by confronting whatever lies beneath—be it our guilt for wanting more money or our mismanaged investments or our less-than-impressive plans for getting rich—once we give it attention and untangle it, we empower ourselves to end the torture. Our attempt to avoid pain backfires on us all the time. We don't want to feel the shame and weirdness we have about getting rich, so we stay broke and constantly feel shame and weirdness when it comes to our lack of money. We don't want to feel the stress involved with managing large amounts of money, so we remain broke and are constantly stressed out about money. We don't want to make money a central focus of our lives because we feel other things are so much more important, so we remain broke and out of touch with our finances and, as a result, we are constantly worrying/thinking about money, almost more than anything else.

........................................................

The very unfunny cosmic joke: In an attempt
to protect ourselves from pain, we perpetuate
behaviors that create the very pain we are
trying to avoid.

........................................................

Thanks to our love of avoidance, the average person spends more time figuring out which is the perfect angle to take the hottest selfie from than she does figuring out what she really wants out of life, how much that will cost, and how to increase her income in order to make that happen. I personally bitched and moaned for decades about how broke I was, how frustrated I was, and how I couldn't see a way out. But my attention span when it came to actually getting specific about the money I required, applying myself, committing to learning new skills, or taking big risks was literally nonexistent. I was Her Royal Highness of Denial. I had no idea what my monthly nut was or what I was bringing in every month; I just sort of squeezed my eyes shut, held on tight, and hoped I'd wake up at the end of the month with phone service. I, like many people, toiled away as a freelance writer because "that's what I did" and "that's all I knew how to do to make money." Instead of scrambling to find more writing gigs, my time would have been much better spent stepping back, doing the math, and accepting that I was in a complete dead-end situation: Twenty-four hours in a day + just me writing + charging forty dollars an hour = I'm tired, grouchy, and a really bad tipper.

We're taught that if we keep working harder, somehow the money will come. If this was true, all rich people would be bloodshot and gasping for air instead of sailing around on yachts. When we focus on the money instead of working ourselves to death, and get mighty clear about how much we desire to make and what we can do differently in order to make it happen, we open the door to new freedoms.

..............................................................................

The number one thing that holds people back is
resisting change.

..............................................................................

You have to be willing to change something if you want
to change your financial situation. It's that simple. You may
have to put your ego aside and ask for help from a mentor or
a coach, you may have to take a job that isn't your dream job
as a stepping-stone to get you where you're going, you may
have to triple your rates, make sales calls to people who've
never heard of you, spend money you're scared to spend, take
a job where you feel like you have no idea what the hell
you're doing and figure it out as you go along. If you're playing it safe and you want to be rich, you need to stop playing
it safe. You need to shift your focus from where you're at and
what you stand to lose and become consumed by thoughts of
where you desire to be and all you have to gain. You need to
play to win instead of play not to lose.

For example, I know someone who's got a steady, good-
paying job that is the most boring job on the planet (in his
words). He does media training on the side, which he loves,
and the side business is booming with very little effort on his
part—he's so good, word of mouth has gotten him more
work than he can handle. He actually has to turn people away
because he doesn't have the time to take on new clients and
keep his day job at the same time.

He desperately wants to make more money and do what
he loves but feels stuck—he'll never get more than a 3 percent

raise a year at his day job and only has so much time to work with media training clients on the side. Of course, he could summon forth his mighty inner warrior, quit his day job, leap bravely into building his own business, and make millions doing media training. But he doesn't even see this as a possibility because he's buying into the fears and beliefs that *only an idiot would quit a steady job for the unknown. He's not ready, the economy could tank at any minute, what if he doesn't make as much doing media training full time as he does at his day job, etc.* Of course, there are no guarantees that he will flourish if he takes the leap, but he's fairly guaranteed to spend the majority of his precious days on Earth waking up at his day job with his face on his desk and a keyboard imprint on his cheek if he doesn't.

The story goes that when Columbus first came to the New World, the natives didn't see his fleet of ships right away even though they were standing right there on the beach looking out at them. They'd never seen a ship before; people floating on water was a completely foreign concept to them and it took time for their brains to connect the dots and absorb what appeared before them. So, at first, they literally saw nothing but ocean.

This is where so many people get stuck when trying to figure out what to do to make money—they're trying to change their lives from the perspective of their current reality. The new opportunities are so foreign to them that they can't see them or they just don't make any damn sense.

....................................................................

Change your mind, change your life.

....................................................................

I'm going to touch on five different scenarios to help you maximize your income stream, but I want you to keep in mind that no matter whatcha got goin', you have to expand your mindset beyond where you're at if you really want to knock it out of the park. Wake up, become aware of how you're perceiving "reality," make new choices, get outside help for fresh perspective, believe in the unbelievable. Most people stay in financial struggle not because they suck at what they do or don't have any prospects, but because they don't stretch their minds.

Regardless of which of these scenarios applies to you, read them all because there's always some overlap, and you never know where you'll get the spark for an idea that will change your life:

1. YOU START YOUR OWN BUSINESS.

    I've been an entrepreneur for over two decades and can't imagine living any other way, but it's definitely not for everyone. Here are some pros and cons my tribe and I discuss on the reg:

    **Pros:**
    - There's no limit to how much money you can make or how big you can grow your business. Small, medium, or large, the choice is yours. The decision is yours. The oyster is yours.

    - You design your own lifestyle, work when and how you want and with whom you want. You might travel the world while running your business, run it out of your kitchen, only hire your pals, work in your robe, whatevs.

- You're the boss. The decisions are yours, the victories are yours, the rule that everyone has to bring his dog to work is yours.

**Cons:**
- You're the boss. The responsibilities are yours, the risks are yours, the ass on the line is yours.

- You have no structure but the structure you create yourself, so your discipline must be rock solid.

- Oftentimes, especially at the beginning, you are alone. In front of your computer. A lot. Which is why the mandatory bringing your dog to work rule is very helpful.

If you decide to go into business for yourself:

- Notice what excites you, what comes naturally to you, what you're excited to share with the world, whose product or service turns you on and inspires you to do or make something similar. Get as many specifics in place as you can and see if you can make a business out of it.

- Another great way to get ideas is by noticing a complaint you often hear yourself or other people talking about: *There are no cute and functional bags to carry my laptop around in. How come there are no healthy fast-food options? I'd love to go on a road trip and not eat like crap. When is someone going to write a self-help book that uses jokes and curse words?* Make a list of all the things you can think of that are missing—both products and services. Once you've written them all down, see if there's one that excites you that you could turn into a business filling a need that you know is there.

■ **Do your numbers.** Make sure your idea has profit and growth potential. I've seen so many people start businesses they're superpsyched about that either make hardly any money or wind up costing them money because they were more focused on their enthusiasm than the revenue streams. Both are obviously important, but if you want a hobby, get a hobby. If you want a business that makes money, be clear on how much you desire to make and how you're going to make it. *Do what you love and the money will follow* works well on a throw pillow, but doesn't do much for the bank account.

I'm not a big believer in business plans unless you're going for a loan—business plans are large, daunting, and can make the most determined person be like, *Screw it, maybe I'll go back to school for art history instead*—but I am big on getting clear on, and writing down, all the income possibilities, expenses, projections, target market, etc., for your business. Which you can do on one or two pages. The simpler the better.

- Leverage your time as much as possible. There is only one of you and only so much time in a day, so if you're doing a brick-and-mortar store or in-person work-shops, can you sell/do them online, where you have unlimited access to an unlimited audience? Can you eventually hire people under you to do what you do? Can you provide your service to groups as well as one-on-one? Can you sell information products as well as showing up live? Leveraging your time allows you to work less and make more and all the successful kids are doing it.

- Focus on one thing. Do not try to start two projects at once or fragment your focus or time in any way. Entrepreneurs are usually really creative people, which is awesome when you have to write an entire album or thirty-five marketing e-mails, but can be a menace when you're starting a business. I guaran-tee you, the moment you get a great idea for a busi-ness and start working on it, you'll get awesome ideas for several others. If you split your attention and try to pursue more than one at once, you're screwed. They say a plane uses about 40 percent of its fuel at takeoff. You need all your energy and fo-cus to get the sucker off the ground. Once your new business is up and running, it's still work, of course, but you've gained some momentum and can then look to your other ideas. However, until you are fully up and running and profitable, you are unauthorized to start any other businesses or take on any other huge projects.

- Do whatever it takes. I had a friend who I worked with back in my record company days who was hell-bent on starting her own branding firm. Her day job as a creative director at the record company was taking up all her time so she quit and decided to get a bar-tending job while she got her dream firm up and run-ning. The only job she could find was at a bar right across the street from the company she'd just quit working for.

..................................................................

You can have your ego or you can have your dreams.

..................................................................

She sucked it up, served Jägermeister shots to in-terns who once worked under her, and went on to make many millions with her own business.

- Get good at sales. Sorry, but if you're in business, you're in the business of sales, cuz without sales, you ain't got no business. Take courses, discover the parts about sales that you're good at (it goes deeper than you think), practice, get good at the skill sets, and stop saying how much you love everything about your busi-ness except the sales part.

## 2. YOU HAVE YOUR OWN BUSINESS AND WANT TO GROW IT.

- Hire a coach and/or get a mentor. Are you sick of me saying this yet? Coaches and mentors can see those opportunities that I've spent this whole book screaming and yelling about—the ones that are outside your field of vision because you're in the forest and can't see for the trees. Coaches and mentors are farther along than you are, they're sitting on the top of the mountain, eating an orange, watching you stumble around down there. They can point something out in, oh, twenty-eight seconds, that might take you the next three years to figure out.

- Get clear on which part of your business is bringing in the most revenue. Is it live events? Is it products? Is it high-priced one-on-one stuff? Figure it out and up your game in that area.

- Delegate anything that you haven't yet delegated. A big problem for many entrepreneurs is we get caught working *in* our businesses instead of *on* them. We're so wrapped up in the day to day that taking time to develop new ideas and expand seems like a luxury. It's not. Growth is one of the most exciting and vital parts of your business. Stop pretending you have to do everything yourself, grab your wallet, take a big leap, and hire some more help.

- Seek out partnerships, joint ventures, investors, and other people who can help you grow.

- Look to see where you can create passive income streams (work once, make money forevah). Can you film yourself giving a seminar and sell it as a DVD or a download? Write a book? Create other types of products? Invest in other people's companies? Passive income = the bomb diggity because this is how money flows into your bank account while you're sipping margaritas on a beach.

3. YOU HAVE A JOB YOU HATE/ARE BORED TO DEATH BY.

- Because you are unauthorized to hate/be bored by the thing you spend most of your waking hours doing, you must quit. But before you quit, be grateful to this job that is supporting you and leading you toward your dream job. Also, see number 5 in this section.

4. YOU HAVE A JOB YOU LIKE BUT DON'T MAKE MUCH MONEY.

- Ask for a raise. Get clear on why you believe you deserve this raise, list off all the many contributions you've made to the company and the reasons why you're such an irreplaceable asset. Investigate how your participation has increased the company's revenue, morale, image, reputation as having the most rockin' holiday parties, etc. Do you have more skills, ideas, and strengths to offer the company that they haven't yet taken advantage of or aren't aware of? Maybe you can work with your boss to map out a time frame and a path to a promotion?

Figure out what amount of money you feel you're worth, ask for it with confidence and gratitude, and be prepared to walk if you don't get it. The reality is that when you work for someone else, they set the ceiling on what you can make, so if they're not budging and you're unhappy, it might be time to seek out another company or organization that pays better. Staying where you are and being bitter is not an option.

- Seek out promotions on your own. Are there opportunities within your company that interest you that pay higher salaries? If so, talk to people in those positions and find out who's in charge, what's entailed, and make it your mission to move up. See if you can be of help in any way to them right now, stay in touch, work for them on weekends, endear yourself to them, bake them cookies, show them that you're not screwing around. If your company doesn't promote from within, again, you're at the mercy of how it does business so this may not be an option, but if it is, go for it whole hog.

- Learn all about your industry and find out if people are making more money doing what you do somewhere else. If so, do all the things listed in number 5 below and get yourself a job at another company that pays better.

- Design your own job. If you see things in your company that need doing that aren't being done, create a new job for yourself. Come up with an excellent pitch about all the ways this will benefit the company and help them make craploads of money, and name your salary. You never know, stranger things have happened.

- See if you can switch from getting paid a salary to getting paid by commission. Salary has a ceiling, commissions don't.

- Supplement your income. Find something else you enjoy doing that's lucrative and do that on the side. I'm not talking about being stressed out and overworked, but if you absolutely love your job and your pay isn't getting doubled anytime soon, you have to suck it up and stay at the income level you're at, quit, or figure out something you can do that will bring in extra cash.

5. YOU'RE UNEMPLOYED AND LOOKING FOR A JOB.

- Write down all the specifics that are important to you about your dream job: How much money you make, what kind of people work with you and/or for you, which skills you use in your job, what you wear to work, how it feels going to work, do they have free bagel

Thursdays every week, etc. Make your dream job so real you can see it and, most important, feel it. Meditate on this image and this feeling day and night, be grateful that it exists, have rock-solid faith that it's on its way toward you, and watch your mouth. No nonsense like: *It's so hard to find work, I'm freaking out, the economy sucks, I'm too old, this is taking forever, do I look like I'm about to burst into tears? Is that why nobody is hiring me?* Keep your thoughts, words, beliefs, and feelings aligned with the job you seek and do not stop until you get there.

- Remember that what you're seeking is also seeking you.

- Do every single solitary thing you know to do to get your job—tell every single person you know and every person they know what you're looking for (especially people you're scared to talk to), put your résumé on online job-hunting sites, talk to people who work in your industry and ask for advice and leads, hire a headhunter. Do everything and then do some more—your job is here, you cannot have the desire for the job if the job doesn't exist. Keep your faith strong, your frequency high, your gratitude endless, your mind wide open, and your efforts unceasing until it appears.

- Seize the stepping-stones. If the job you're looking for is taking awhile to find you, take the job that leads you closer. It may not be totally perfect, but if it gets you into the world you want to be in—e.g., being the assistant to an agent if you want to be an agent, working in an ad agency as a secretary if you want to be a copywriter, working at a restaurant in the fashion district of your city if you want to get into fashion, anything that will put you in contact with the people you want to meet and/or the skill set you need to learn— jump on it. Learn everything you can, meet as many people as you can meet, keep your eye on the prize, and do your best.

Regardless of which path you're on, here are some critical, basic things you need to be doing if you want to get rich:

- Treat money the way you'd like to be treated. You are having a relationship with money and in order for things to go well, you need to put time, focus, and love into this relationship. Give moola a reason to hang out with you. Take an interest in its life.

  - Get clear on how much money you have, what you're bringing in (incomes, investments, royalties, curse jar income from your kids, everything), how much you require each month to live, and where each of your dollars goes. What you focus on you create more of. This will take approximately fifteen minutes in case you're getting ready to reel off into overwhelm/bored-alreadydom.

- Treat money with respect. Pay attention to your money and be grateful for all the awesomeness it brings to your life. Speak highly of it. Give and receive it with glee, gratitude, and generosity. If you see it on the ground, pick it up and give it a good home.

- Hire professionals to help you manage your money if you're feeling confused or overwhelmed or clueless— financial planners, accountants, bookkeepers. Do not ask your broke-ass friends for financial advice! For the love of God, turn to people who know what the hell they're doing.

- Be a good host, make room for your money, make it feel welcome. Nature hates a vacuum, so create space for your new money to fill up. Get a financial planner and set up a retirement fund, investment funds, or a savings account—make it a no-brainer so you have places to put your money when it starts pouring in. If you've never made much money before, it can feel overwhelming and confusing to know what to do with it once you have it, and your panic could cause you to psychically repel it. Prepare the nest and you'll be more confident, and excited, to get rich. This could take fifteen minutes on the phone (and costs you nothing up front—financial planners work on percentage).

- Don't take failure personally. Get your ego out of it and your curiosity into it. Approach failure with an attitude of *Hmmm, I wonder why that happened? Was there something I could have done differently?* Don't fall into the trap of creating an award-winning drama around failure and using it as proof that you're a moron/doomed/never gonna get what you want. If you have the desire to get rich, the way is there.

..............................................................

Temporary failure becomes permanent defeat only when you say so.

..............................................................

- Hem not, haw not. Take action on your desires right now. You must head down your path to riches with a sense of urgency or else you'll fall prey to distractions, laziness, limiting beliefs, procrastination, binge watching TV shows. Work with diligent focus and grateful expectation, do all you can every day to the best of your ability, remember that the sooner you achieve your financial goals, the longer you get to spend on Earth basking in your riches.

  - IMPORTANT URGENCY NOTE: Urgency is the opposite of hurrying. Hurrying comes from lack and a sense of panic that there isn't enough to go around. It leads to feeling overwhelmed, and making mistakes, and inspires comparison and competition with your fellow humans. When you rush, you're in a state of stress and worry, and you're inclined to maybe do things like spread nasty rumors about others or put gum on the competition's chair. In other words, hurrying lowers your frequency. Urgency, meanwhile, raises you up, gives you energy, focus, and drive. Urgency is the stuff of *I believe my desired life exists, now, so I'm gonna go ahead and carpe my diem*. Stay connected to your Why, get the fuck on the fuck, participate in things that rev you up, hang out with ass kickers . . . you know the drill.

- Charge what you're worth. Money is an energy that comes and goes, ebbs and flows. When you sell a product or service in exchange for money, the person who's paying you is not suddenly thrown into lack. *Whelp, that money's gone for good!* They have the opportunity to benefit from what you've offered, and because you're awesome and gave them something of great value, their investment raises their frequency, which will open them up to receive things of high frequency, including more money. Whatever you offer—music, hilarity, clothes, medical skills, food, managerial services, tax preparation, scented candles—all of it counts. Charge what you and your products are worth. Don't be cheap with others or yourself. Don't be a weirdo about it. Get in the flow.

- Treat everything and everyone with respect and do your best no matter what. An opportunity (or dare I say, a person) that seems really simple and stupid could open the door to huge possibilities. What you put out is mirrored back to you, so if you want greatness, exude greatness. Plus being mean, snobby, and dismissive is lame, so, you know, stay away from that crap.

### SUCCESS STORY: IF SHE CAN DO IT, SO CAN YOU.

*Linda, 50, now owns a marketing agency that bills $1.5 million annually and her only formal education is cosmetology school:*

I started my career as a cosmetologist and now I'm an expert in marketing/legal compliance. I own a marketing agency and we bill $1.5 million annually in services. I always believed I would be successful, even when I opted for beauty school over college.

My personal motto is: "Limitations are self-imposed." One of my best friends passed away when we were in our early twenties. I was determined not to squander my life. My friend would never have a chance at life, so I decided to dive into things with full conviction. I outworked everyone and would do whatever it took to get a job done. In the early days, I would work sixteen-hour days without blinking. I would "shadow" senior management on my day off to learn more. I watched how deals were negotiated and gained knowledge far beyond my title and pay level. I pictured myself running the meetings and cutting the deals. I didn't do vision boards, etc.—but I pictured myself as a successful professional.

I was actually very successful as a hairdresser, but I knew it wasn't what I wanted to do. I saved my money so I had a buffer to last a few months, packed my car, and moved 1,500 miles away from home. Everyone told me I was crazy. The move led me to a job as a VIP tour guide at Universal Studios. I had the pleasure of spending the day with countless celebs, movie executives, and CEOs. The funny thing is, I was busted broke! Doing hair paid much better. I used my vantage point as a tour guide to pinpoint a marketing department where I thought I could be a good fit. Boom— Special Events . . . I basically got to throw parties for a living. With time, my salary steadily increased.

I never doubted that I would be a success. The thought of failure never crossed my mind. Simply believe and be willing to work hard, REALLY hard, to overcome obstacles. If you don't believe success is possible, it isn't. I defied all the odds. Harvard-educated lawyers ask me for my opinion. Sometimes I chuckle to myself—if they only knew my formal education stopped at cosmetology school!

## TO GET RICH

Suggested Money Mantra (say it, write it, feel it, own it):

*I love money because it gives me freedom and options and that's how I love living my life, with a whole lotta freedom and options.*

1. Do your numbers. Get clear on how much money you desire to make and by when (be specific about what the money is for and don't forget to include your monthly nut of bare-necessity costs). Make sure this number is real and connected to specific things that bring up specific emotions. Then chunk it back—if your goal is five years away, chunk it back to how much you will make in four years, how much you will make in two years, how much you need to make this year, in six months, etc., all the way back to this month. Then put a definite plan in place with clear action steps that go toward your goal.

   - Always stay attached to your Why so when things get tough you keep going.

   - Always pay attention to your numbers. If you don't make your financial goal one week, add it on to the next. Your numbers MUST be nonnegotiable or else you'll never get rich.

   - Get organized. Put it all on the schedule instead of just hoping it gets done.

   - Keep your eyes open for new, scary opportunities that may lead to the riches you're seeking.

2. Get educated. Learn as much as you can about how to make more money in whatever business you're in. Investigate what other people in your industry are doing, people who are more financially successful than you are, and follow suit.

3. Hire a coach. Olympic athletes at the top of their games have coaches. Broke people at the bottom of their games insist they can get rich without any help. Just sayin'. Start by writing down all the specific attributes you want in a coach, i.e., specializes in helping people make money, has been through the financial ringer themselves and emerged victorious, lives nearby and can work in person, is a little scary, works one-on-one, etc. Get clear on who you're looking for and what's important to you, and stay open to everyone who presents themselves. Put the word out that you're looking to hire a coach, tell everyone you know and don't know that you're looking, search for coaches online, and if someone looks interesting, get on her mailing lists, attend her seminars, read her books, blogs, social media posts, testimonials. Do everything you can think of to find the perfect coach and trust that when the student is ready, the teacher appears.

4. Open up a new savings account, open a money market account, build the nest, and welcome in all the money that is coming your way.

Please fill in the blank:

I'm grateful to money because _____.

# CHAPTER 11

# YOUR INNER WEALTH

W ay back in the early 1980s, Prince, who was not a huge somebody at the time, was invited to warm up for the Rolling Stones, who were extremely huge somebodies at the time. It was a big break for him and I imagine he was superexcited about it, but when he took the stage wearing nothing but a trench coat and tight black bikini undies, he got booed. Like real loudly. And a lot. A lot, as in they didn't stop booing until he left the stage. Also, they threw stuff at him. And called him names.

At the Rolling Stones' next show, Prince once again pranced out in his skivvies and was received with the same verbose lack of enthusiasm by the Stones' fans. Only this time—as he left the stage amidst a sea of boos and snickers—he made a decision. He did not decide at that moment, as many people would have, that perhaps he should spend the following afternoon shopping for pants. Prince instead decided, *Screw these idiots, this ain't who I am or what I'm about.* Prince decided that instead of conforming to what everyone else expected of him and trying to win over people who didn't appreciate who he was, that he would never, ever, be anyone's warm-up act again. Not even the freaking Rolling Stones.

All I can say is there were some monster cojones tucked into those little black panties of his.

Yes, Prince was one of the most talented musical badasses to ever parade around the Earth. And guess what? You have gifts and talents just as unique and important inside of you. And you're meant to respect, nurture, and strut your youness as unapologetically as Prince strutted his. The more in tune and in love you are with your awesome self, the less crap you will give about what any nonfans of yours think, the easier it will be to strut your strut, find your joy, and get it on with the green goodness of money.

This is because getting rich, and succeeding at making any of your other dreams a reality, depends on who you're being: how you're thinking, speaking, believing, imagining, stretching, perceiving your world—all of which affect how you act. When you love and connect deeply with your highest self, you'll discover that your insecurities about sucking at your job or your fears about your money running out or your anger about the tomato that just hit you in the face while on stage—none of that is who you are. That gnarliness is just where you're at.

As a human being, you will always face challenges and fears and sit next to someone who chews with their mouth open. We grow and learn through friction, even friction within ourselves, so your job isn't to try to rid your life of uncomfortable moments or prickly challenges or hard, long looks in the mirror. Your job is to master the art of responding, aka being response-able for, and aware of, your thoughts and actions. Your job is to short-circuit your knee-jerk instinct to react, which will keep you playing out the same tired old low-frequency patterns you've been lugging around your whole life. Acting out the same old impulses is why people go on a diet and lose a ton of weight only to put it back on again, why people who win the lottery eventually end up right back where they started financially, why most New Year's resolutions are barely even a memory by February. If you only change on the exterior and work on things outside yourself (cutting down on your donut intake), but you're being the same person on the inside with the same mindset of lack and fear, e.g., *if I can't hide behind my wall of flab I will be seen, and vulnerable, and very possibly rejected*, you won't evolve.

Step back for a moment and acknowledge the fact that you're alive. There was a time before you were alive, and there will be a time when you're no longer alive. But right now, you are participating in the confoundingly glorious cartoon called Life on Earth. The life force known as Universal Intelligence is flowing through your meaty human body, making your blood pump, your mind think, your heart desire, your intuition tell you to look behind the toaster for the car keys you've spent half the afternoon searching for. This force that flows through you is the essence of who you are, it's the highest frequency there is—you are Universal Intelligence seeking expression on Earth through the you that is you. You are a valuable and irreplaceable asset to the Universe. You are mighty beyond comprehension. You are a badass.

Let us not forget that money is currency and currency is energy. So when your energy is vibrating at the highest frequency possible—the frequency of love—you're like a freaking tornado of awesomeness, swirling up all the goodness and riches around you and showering them right back out into the world for the benefit of everyone you touch. If you wanna get rich, understand that just by being you, you have already struck gold.

Grab a cup of chamomile tea, light a vanilla candle, and let's get down to some of the best ways to get it on with your big beautiful self so you can start making some money around here.

## MEDITATION

Sitting in purposeful silence is food for your heart and soul. It's as if your mind spends most of its time hanging out at a loud bar (your brain), where everyone's screaming and yelling and singing "The Wild Rover" at the top of their drunken lungs. Meditation shuts down the bar, rolls everyone out the door, and allows your higher self to commune with Universal Intelligence so they can actually hear each other. You are an energetic creature, and connecting to Universal Intelligence is infinitely empowering, because that bond strengthens your connection to your true self, not the self you've created with years of limiting thoughts and beliefs. Meditation allows you to emotionally connect to the truth that you are an infinitely powerful spirit energy, your reality goes far beyond what your five senses tell you, and you are a badass. You can literally *feel* it. And the more you feel this, the more powerful, happy, and rich you will let yourself be.

Even meditating for five minutes every day can make a profound difference in your life. If you've never done it before, all you do is sit down, focus on your breath, and anytime a thought comes into your mind, you just refocus on your breath. The end. And remember, it's called a meditation practice for a reason—it takes a whole lot of practice to shut off the noise.

..............................................................................

You have infinite greatness inside of you. Let it win over the BS.

..............................................................................

## AFFIRMATIONS

Your environment, and especially the people you surround yourself with, greatly affect how you perceive yourself and your world. The person you spend the most time with affects you the most. And the person you spend the most time with is . . . you. Hence, what you tell yourself on a regular basis is muy importante. All the thoughts, beliefs, and words you've had on repeat throughout your life, either consciously or unconsciously, created the reality you're presently hanging out in. So if you're not loving the reality you're presently hanging out in, you're gonna wanna go ahead and change things up. One of the best ways to reprogram your mindset is through affirmations. Pay attention to what falls out of your mouth and what pops into your mind during meditation, and if it's negative, rewrite it with new words and thoughts that transmit positive feeling, and say these new words over and over and over and over and over. Some options (but only if they bring up feeling in you):

> *Money flows to and from me easily. I love spending it and I love making it.*
>
> *There is plenty of money to go around.*
>
> *Money is freedom, money is power, money is my pal.*
>
> *I love money and money loves me.*
>
> *The money I desire is already here.*
>
> *I am energy, money is energy, we are samesies, we are besties.*

## BE NICE

So simple, so lovely, and yet so challenging when someone is driving below the speed limit in front of you on a one-lane road. Yet as satisfying as it might be in the moment, being an a-hole never feels good, even if the jackass totally had it coming. Losing it makes you feel like crap and, in particular, like crap about yourself. Same thing with saying horrible things about yourself—even if it's intended to get a laugh, ragging on yourself . . . I mean, it's not like you can't hear yourself, you're standing right *there*. If you're all into the self-deprecating hilarity, just think about how it would feel if someone said the stuff you say about yourself to you: *I don't know how it happens, but food just finds its way into your mouth, you're just sitting there and all of a sudden you're like, look at that, I'm chewing on a brick of cheese. You are such an idiot, you'd lose your head if it wasn't attached to your neck.* Not nice, right? So why is it okay if you say these things about yourself? If you can't say something nice, don't say anything at all—the phrase that caused a boom in the kitten-poster industry will cause a boom in your overall happiness and wealth factor. We live in an energetic Universe; what you put out comes right back to you.

## BE PATIENT

Patience is one of the most powerful, and most challenging, traits to develop in our modern world. The more techno-logically advanced we get, the more infuriated we get when we have to wait. At all. For anything. Even for a couple of seconds. Just the other day I was heating up some leftover lasagna, and I put it in the microwave for a minute or so, and it was still cold. So I punched in another thirty seconds and it still wasn't hot enough. I had to wait a whole fifty-five seconds more before it finally got it together and some cheese started melting around here. I swore right then and there that I was going to get a new microwave because this was ridiculous, it shouldn't take that long to heat up noodles. But then, we all know who the ridiculous one really is. Not only was I being ridiculous, I was getting frustrated, angry, and stressed out, which are not only low on the energy totem pole, but lead to real physical dis-ease if you participate in them often enough.

Being patient instead of high strung and freaked out makes you feel a whole lot better because it creates space for you to enjoy life in a way that rushing around blocks out. Patience allows you to notice the feel of the air on your skin, to experience the realization that you have so many people who love you, to be aware that this very moment in time is a miracle that will never, ever happen again. You ain't gonna get any of that while complaining about the idiot at your cell-phone company who's had you on hold for thirty-five minutes. Participating in patience is one of the best ways to love your fabulous self.

Our lives are made up of tiny moments, and in each moment you are making a choice that is either a high-energy choice or a low-energy choice. While my run-in with some cold noodles might seem insignificant, these moments add up to create the whole of the reality you're presently staring in the face. What you do in each tiny moment matters greatly. Shut up, slow down, breathe, connect to your higher self, and act with intention. What you focus on you create more of, and the more tiny thoughts you have that are high frequency, the more high-frequency experiences you'll bring into your life.

## UP YOUR CONFIDENCE

Somewhere along the way we were taught to believe that we're basically screwed in the confidence department if we weren't born with it. We look at someone walk into a party who doesn't know anyone there and he's all cracking jokes, asking everyone if he can grab them something from the bar, chatting up the ladies, leaning against the wall, one ankle casually and confidently crossed over the other. We look at him like *I could just never, ever be like that. I mean, who IS that guy?* Meanwhile, you totally could be like that guy, if you wanted to be. We are all born confident, some of us just get lost along the way and buried beneath things like self-loathing and not wanting to be like your show-off dad who totally ignored you. Or maybe you got yelled at any time you spoke up for yourself so you decided it was safer to hide in the shadows. Confidence, like all other pieces of your mindset, is a muscle. So all you gots to do is exercise your confidence muscle if you want to build it up. Here are my three favorite confidence boosters:

1. Fake yourself out with your bod. It's amazing what gullible creatures we are. Just like stress (over, um, nothing) can cause your body to get sick, sometimes mortally so, your body can trick your mind into believing things too. Which is why if you want to feel more confident, and you hold your body as if you were confident, you feel more confident. Stand up straight, take deep breaths, smile, walk with a strut, hold your head high, give solid, firm handshakes . . . start with your body and your mind will follow suit.

2. Just do it. When my niece was about fifteen she wanted to come visit me in Venice Beach, which meant she had to fly by herself all the way across the country from New York. She was terrified by the thought of navigating two major airports on her own—JFK and LAX—but her mother and I told her she'd never be alone. Her mom would walk her up to the gate and, because she was a minor, a nice person from the airline would get her on the plane and deliver her right to me on the other side. Easy peasy lemon squeezy.

So she feels a bit better about it, and on the big day, as her mother is driving her to the airport, they get stuck in really bad traffic. It's so congested that by the time they arrive there's no time to park, so my sister-in-law just pulls up to the curb, shoves my niece out of the car, and screams *Run! You're gonna miss your flight! Run!* So my niece grabs her stuff, runs inside in a panic, manages to find someone from the airline, and gets herself on the plane.

I will never forget seeing her walk out of the gate area on the other side, head held back, six feet taller, pulling her suitcase like she could swing it around, beat you with it, and steal your car if she felt like it. *I just navigated my way through John F. Kennedy Airport, bitches. Out. Of. My. Way.* If you desire to do something, there is a part of you deep down that knows you're capable or else you wouldn't waste your time thinking about it. Don't wait until you're confident—that's like waiting until you lose the extra five pounds before you'll let yourself go on vacation—just do it. The more you push yourself to do the things you're scared to do, the stronger your confidence muscle will become.

3. Remember you are already large, Marge. You are a spiritual being running around Earth in a physical body. Your desires were given to you when you showed up in human form and those desires are basically Universal Intelligence seeking expression through you. You are here to do whatever it is that you're feeling not so confident about doing. Your desires are your Universal Marching Orders, and there is no wrong outcome. If you can wrap your mind around who you really are (hint: meditate), really wrap your mind around the fact that you are Universal Energy, and think of it often, you will understand why you are such a big freaking deal.

## SERVE OTHERS

The more you give, the more you receive. There ain't no frequency quite like the frequency of a giver. It's right up there with the frequency of the lover. Serving others with your gifts—writing a blog post that helps someone heal from a broken heart, teaching a kid how to read, making a blueberry pie that blows someone's mind—is like giving a big ole gift to yourself. Even little things count, like giving someone directions, thinking nice thoughts about someone (extra points if it's someone you're pissed at), picking up something a stranger dropped and handing it to them, saying the three little words everyone longs to hear: *Want my fries?* The high-frequency energy that goes out when we give always comes back to us. It may or may not come back via the person we gave to, but it absolutely always comes back in some form. We are here to share, we really are, which is why greed doesn't bring joy to anyone. Greed inspires more greed—it's a misaligned method of trying to fill a longing that can only be filled by giving, not by taking. If you want to be happy, make others happy.

## LIGHTEN UP

When you have a crappy attitude, it's usually because you want attention, to be heard, for other people to consider your needs first and foremost: *I was wronged! That guy cut me off! This is hard! It's unfair! Feel sorry for me! Feel my pain!* When you choose freedom and happiness over wanting to be right or to be seen, you win. Get out of victim mode, remember everyone is just as obsessed with themselves and their own feelings as you are with yours, and stop taking everything personally.

## CELEBRATE

If you get a new client, if you get up the nerve to ask someone out, if you get the job, the house, or the last cookie, celebrate. We're so damn busy all the time we rarely take the time out to acknowledge our awesomeness. Meanwhile, what you focus on you create more of, appreciation appreciates, badassery badassifies. Take the time to feel into, be grateful for, and do a cartwheel about all the greatness you're bringing into the world, and you will empower yourself to bring even more.

## FORGIVE

Oy the energy we waste lugging around the wet sandbag of guilt and resentment! It is truly one of the biggest wastes of time, and yet one of the all-time favorite human activities. The past ain't gonna change anytime soon, and being upset at yourself or someone else for something that is done and gone is like refusing to take the trash out. You carry it around as it gets stinkier and stinkier, the fly swarm around you gets thicker and thicker, and all that you desire—happiness, peace, freeing yourself from repeating the crappy experience that you refuse to stop focusing on—will elude you, and will continue to elude you, until you take out the trash.

................................................................

Imperfect = I'm perfect. You're human. You're gonna
screw up. Other humans are gonna screw up. Let it go.

................................................................

We tend to hold on to resentment because we feel like the nitwit who wronged us doesn't deserve forgiveness. Meanwhile, the only person being punished by your resentment is you. Forgiveness is about you deserving peace, not necessarily about others deserving your forgiveness. You are allowing nasty thoughts of nasty things to take up precious space in your mind. If you love yourself, you'll end your own torture and let it go.

Compassion is the key to forgiveness. We act like jerks because we're in pain and fear, not because we're out to ruin the world. We cheat on people we love and make fun of people because we're insecure. We blow people off, show up late, check our texts while a friend is in the middle of telling us how excited she is about her new boyfriend because we're oblivious, checked out, unwilling to engage or be present in life for fear of failing or not being loved or whatever load we're carrying around deep down. Everyone's an asshole and everyone is awesome, we're all all of it. When we're acting unconsciously and not at our highest level, it's because we're in pain and fear. Everyone is fighting his or her own inner battles. Do not define yourself and other people by our less than impressive behaviors. It's the pain speaking, and you can find compassion for a person in pain. If you want to be free, make the choice to forgive.

There's a woman named Louise Hay, who is basically the godmother of self-help. She got her start by writing a book about what she learned when she healed herself from "incurable" cervical cancer via forgiveness, affirmations, visualization, nutrition, and other hippie-type stuff instead of surgery and drugs. She believed she was holding on to resentment from childhood rape and abuse and figured if she could choose to hold on to it, she could also choose to let it go. Within six months she was cured, and she went on to help countless people cure themselves of all sorts of dis-ease through the almighty practice of self-love.

Poverty and staying broke are diseases that we cause with our mindsets, which is why when we make the conscious choice to focus on what's true for us and what feels good, instead of why we can't and mustn't get rich, we can cure ourselves.

..........................................................

Self-love means doing things that make
you feel good.

..........................................................

I know that sounds like a no-brainer, but think about how
often we do things that make us feel incredibly not good—
we do it all the damn time! We tell ourselves we can't have
what we want because it's too risky, we're too inexperienced,
that person is out of our league, we drink too much, marry
morons, stay in jobs we hate . . . I could fill up the next forty-
five pages. My point is: Become more aware of what makes
you feel good, and go do that. Always check in with your
feelings before doing or saying anything. Practice responding
to situations according to how they make you feel instead of
reacting based on old beliefs and fears. Pay attention to yourself, your awesome, adorable, imperfect self, and make the
conscious effort to give yourself what you need, including all
the riches you desire. You will love yourself for it.

## TO GET RICH

Suggested Money Mantra (say it, write it, feel it, own it):
   *I love money because it lets me be the most me I can be.*

1. Meditate for at least five minutes a day. No need to ask any
   questions beforehand, just sit in silence and connect.

2. Use the affirmations in this chapter, or your favorites that you've come up with while doing the work in this book, and commit to three that specifically speak to raising your appreciation of yourself and of money. Write them every morning and every night, say them all day long, take them with you wherever you go, and feel into them.

3. Go out of your way every day to do at least three nice things for people. Also, when you're about to be not nice, breathe, pause, and make a different choice.

4. Practice patience. Notice when you're getting uptight or grouchy and remember: You can't rush the Universe. Don't try to pull open the flower. It all blooms according to plan. Breathe, relax, stay the course, and lighten up.

5. Walk tall, sit up straight, practice using your body to become more confident.

6. Go on the Internet and do a search for the following text: *Our Deepest Fear* by Marianne Williamson. Print it out, tape it to your refrigerator, and read it as often as possible.

Please fill in the blank:
I'm grateful to money because _____.

# CHAPTER 12

# TENACITY

I used to live next door to a lady who worked in finance, who decided to start her own investment management company. She took a huge leap of faith and put up her entire life savings to get it off the ground, because, unlike most people who start businesses like hers, she didn't have a wealthy backer or piles of cash to burn. She had to go to da hip (reach for her wallet) and empty out every last cent. She had two kids in diapers the week she launched her company, one of whom was in the hospital at the time. And, because the Universe is hilarious, she also had jury duty.

Add to all of this that she was working in finance—an industry that doesn't have a whole lot of skirts walking around in it. It was not only challenging being a woman, but it was also challenging being small beans—she told me that at the very beginning of her journey, when she was looking for her first investors, she was on the phone with a prospect who looked at what she had invested so far (her entire life savings) and said, "Is that all you've got?" He passed, she hung up, burst into tears, totally humiliated, and started freaking out about whether or not she'd be able to pull this off, to provide all the things she wanted for her family, to have the freedom to work for herself, and to not lose every dime she had.

I used to see her walking down our street in a daze, white as pancake batter, pounds lighter every time, a ghost. I'd ask her how it was going and she'd always say, "Hanging in there!" Meanwhile, the question I really wanted to ask her is if I could make her a meatball sandwich—I was honestly a little worried about her. I could tell the stress was seriously taking its toll, and when I moved away she was still wandering the streets, still waiting for her business to either make it or crash, still somehow not blowing away in the wind.

I talked to her about a year later and was thrilled to hear that she'd resumed her ability to speak in complete sentences in a tone above a whisper, and that her business—after teetering on the edge for nearly a year—was totally kicking ass. Today, the Zombie Next Door has increased her net worth by roughly twenty times. Twenty times, y'all! She works only with people she loves, she takes great care of her family, and she never would have gotten there if she hadn't stuck with it. And come up with the perfect story to get out of jury duty.

Here are some key mindset pieces she had in place that helped her take the leap and stay the course as she trudged through the Valley of Darkness that first year:

**She held tight to her Why.** She wanted the money and success for the freedom it gave her, to take care of her family, to prove to herself that she could do it. Also, she wasn't terribly psyched about the prospect of losing her entire life savings if the business tanked.

**She went to the spiritual gym.** She constantly read books by other entrepreneurs, she had pictures taped to her walls of women who'd done stuff like run successful restaurants in war zones, she memorized poems, meditated, and constantly reminded herself that uncertainty is part of the process. Everyone has to fling themselves into the unknown to get to the next level—she wasn't a drama queen about it.

**She did her homework.** She studied her industry, the people she'd love to work with, and learned creative ways to sell by finding common ground between herself and prospects that were "out of her league." Once she landed her second big investor using her new badass sales skills, her business started flying.

**She got a mentor.** It was 2008, all these other much bigger firms were crashing down around her, and she was brought to the point where she didn't think she could take it anymore, so she sought out a mentor who gave her great advice: He told her to

> go surfing. To take it day by day, that nobody wins
> if you quit—it will feel good in the moment but
> then it's over. If your investors are going to fire you,
> let them fire you, don't fire yourself. Never give up.

The number one thing wealthy people attribute their success to is tenacity. Nobody achieves great success without walking through the fire. And the difference between those who succeed and those who fail is a no-nonsense commitment to staying the course no matter how hot the fire gets. There is almost always a moment when all hell breaks loose—you lose a key client, your storeroom burns down, Starbucks moves in across the street from the coffee shop you just opened—and in these moments you have two choices: You can either say *Screw it, I'm out of here,* or *Is that all you got, sucka?* When the pain is almost too much to bear, if your mindset is weak, you will give up and blame something or someone else for your failure. If your mindset is rock solid, you will persevere. Here are some key ways to keep going no matter how sucky the going gets:

## PUSH IT REAL GOOD

I went on a rafting trip down the Colorado River, and a friend of mine and I had to hike up from the very bottom of the Grand Canyon afterward to get back to my car. We ended up getting off the river a bit later than expected, which meant we had to haul ass the entire eight-hour hike up the side of the canyon if we were going to make it before the sun went down.

While still on the raft, I had visions of a leisurely hike up, stopping every so often to take a dip in the stream that ran beside us for the first few hours of the climb, taking selfies to impress everyone far and wide that I'd hiked the mother of all canyons, and, most important, resting. A lot. I was a far cry from what one would call in shape, which is why, when we finally neared the top of the Grand Canyon as the sun was setting, I was wobbly kneed, exhausted, and not altogether sure I was going to make it the final quarter mile without soiling myself. I remember, as I was begging my body to keep it together while chanting my mantra, *Almost there, almost there*, I heard my friend yelling a word that I knew I understood but that did not register right away. I turned around to look at her and saw that she was pointing up the hill to the bus that had just pulled up. The bus that would take us back to our car, parked several miles away. The bus that only came every forty-five minutes. It was then that I realized the word she was screaming was *Run!*

If, moments before all this, someone suddenly appeared on the trail with a clipboard and a survey and asked me if it was possible for me to run at that very moment, my answer would have been absolutely not, and not just because I don't think I can, but because it's physically impossible. However, if the clipboard person had promised that, if by some miracle I could muster up a run, I'd be rewarded with a place to sit down, a cheeseburger, a beer, and the first shower I'd had in over a week, my answer would have been different. So, with my sights set on not sitting on a bench in the dark for forty-five minutes, sweaty, filthy, starving, dying for a tub of moisturizer, I did the impossible and ran the rest of the way up the hill and made the bus.

We all have habitual places where we stop—a certain threshold where something gets too intimate or too expensive or too close to success for our comfort. Crossing this threshold is exactly what we need to do to exit our comfort zones and transform our lives, which is why it's so terrifying to us and why our subconscious minds gather all the king's horses and all the king's men to make sure we run away, run away! We're usually totally oblivious to this stopping point, and have a lifetime's worth of excellent excuses we use to back our way out of greatness, i.e., *I'm not scared of investing in myself, but that class is way out of my price range* or *I just realized I don't want to write this book that I've been working on for years and am almost done with, I want to write a different one.* If you've made the decision to make the kind of money you've never made before, blasting through this terror threshold is critical. So keep an eye out for the rallying cry to retreat, understand that you have arrived at the magical door to the other side, focus on this truth instead of the desire to get into bed and read magazines, and break on through to the other side.

## RISK BEING UNPOPULAR

Successful people are tenacious, which means they keep the faith much longer than the average person does. Because of this, the average person tends to look upon the successful person, before they have become successful, as insane, ridiculous, give it a rest already! Successful people must hold tight to their vision while everyone around them is shouting things like (if you're, say, Thomas Edison), *What do you think you are, magic? You're never gonna get that stupid thing to light up. Go get a job!*

I remember seeing one of the most impressive displays of tenacity on a flight once while waiting for my plane to take off. A woman came bursting on with her two sons just as they were closing the doors with that sweaty, disheveled, wild-eyed look specific to two types of people: out of shape people who've just narrowly made their flight, and people who have just killed someone. We're all sitting there, a captive audience strapped into our chairs, watching her try to find a place for their luggage in the overhead compartments, deal with getting the kids in their seats, and apologize to the entire plane for the holdup. She obviously booked the flight last minute too, because they weren't sitting together, they each had middle seats, one in front of the other, which made it even more difficult for her to get everyone settled.

But her real difficulty was with her older son, who refused to sit down. He was about nine years old, and as he watched his little brother climb into his middle seat, he quietly informed his mother that he wanted a window seat. She responded with something about him being out of luck and that he needed to sit down right now, to which he calmly replied, "No, I'm sitting by the window," to which she hissed, "Sit down," to which he said, "No," to which she shot another apologetic look down the aisle to the crowd. I'm sitting there, in my window seat, watching all this, trying to figure out if I should give him my seat and end her torture, give him a talking to, or hire him as my coach. I'd never seen such unshakable, calm resolve in the face of such great danger—an entire airplane full of pissed off grown-ups. Yet this kid, without being bratty or pitching a fit, held his ground until the guy in front of me got up and switched seats with him.

His desire for, and vision of, his goal outweighed and blinded him to all other options: public humiliation, verbal abuse from adults other than his mother, no screen time for the rest of his life. He had the stick-to-itiveness to pooh-pooh one of the biggest blocks to success known to man: the need to be liked and fit in. If you plan on going from poor to rich, you too must stick to your guns at the risk of being unpopular. You cannot make this big change in your life and expect nothing around you to change, especially your relationships with other people. When you change who you're being, you will upset people, you will lose friends, and maybe even cause rifts with family members, so your desire to grow into who you're meant to be must be firmly placed in the very front of your mind at all times—as must the specifics of the life you're creating for yourself and the feelings associated with it, so you have the courage to stay the course. Trust that you're meant to realize your desires, and know that while you'll still love the people you lose along the way, you will attract new people who are at the same frequency you are.

## IGNORE THE TRIXTERS

When you make the no-nonsense decision to change your life and get rich, your subconscious is not only going to fling all your worst fears in your face, but it will also present you with what I call trixters. Trixters are superjuicy temptations, custom made by your Little Prince to knock you off track and back into your comfort zone.

I have a client who decided to quit her job in public relations and open her own firm. She was excited to be her own boss, to make her own hours, and to rake in as much money as she set her mind to. She lives in a small town where there aren't a whole lot of client possibilities and even fewer good job prospects, and a week after she quit her day job she got an offer to work for one of the only other PR companies in town. It was a sweet deal, and part of her was terrified that if she turned it down and went out on her own she wouldn't get enough clients to survive, let alone thrive. But she stuck to her guns, said no to the job, and *the very next day* she got seven, I am not exaggerating, seven calls from people who wanted to hire her as their publicist.

Universal Intelligence gave you your desires with the purpose of having you carry them out. When you align your energy, actions, and mindset to bring them forth, the Universe gets on board. When you decide to get rich, you must be laser focused on your decision and your emotional reasons for making money, because it's a matter of when, not if, things, people, and events will show up to tempt you away from your goal. Success is all about letting the trixters pass you by so you can seize the opportunities that are lining up behind them.

## FORM SUCCESSFUL HABITS

When we think of habits, we usually think of things like biting your nails, smoking, cursing, twirling your hair, getting up early to walk the dog, yelling when you talk on your cell phone, etc. Meanwhile, habits make up the majority of our behaviors: Laziness is a habit, feeling overwhelmed is a habit, being late is a habit, failure is a habit, success is a habit, patience is a habit, gossiping is a habit, making money is a habit, being broke is a habit. Because a habit is any behavior you do automatically and repeatedly without really thinking about it, most things we do fall into the habit category because most of us ain't thinking so much. As we've seen, we're usually in a state of re-acting to our subconscious beliefs. Once we become aware and decide to consciously re-spond instead, we can change our habits, which will change our realities.

We've spent loads of time working on changing your habits around how you think, believe, and speak, and because habits are so major, I want to give you a few more tips. But first, here are some habits you're going to want to develop if you haven't already. These are some of the most common habits of successful people. Successful people:

Take risks

Stick to their decisions

Set good boundaries

Give back

Work smart

Go to the spiritual gym (read self-help books, exercise, meditate, work with mastermind groups, etc.)

Delegate

Constantly learn

Stay disciplined

Focus

Practice patience

Surround themselves with ass kickers

Talk about ideas, not other people

Get back up instead of give up

Show up on time

Know what's going on around them

Know what's going on with their money

It's all stuff we've been talking about, but it's important to be aware of the fact that all of these things are habits. So if you've got bad habits that are blocking you from developing these good habits, make the conscious effort to disrupt your flow and get going on new ones. Here are some of my favorite tips for doing that:

1. Have zero tolerance for negotiations. Perhaps my best tip when it comes to forming new habits is to remove yourself from the negotiation process. Let's say you've decided you're going to get into the habit of making five sales calls before lunch every day. Right before you're

about to dial the phone, the idea pops into your head to check Facebook one more time to see if anyone commented on the picture you posted of your grandmother in a wet suit. The moment that thought comes into your head, you recognize it as what it is: a negotiation away from your goal. "I'm just gonna go on Facebook for one little minuteypoo." Or if you've quit drinking it might be, "Maybe I'll just have one little sip." Or if you're meditating, "Maybe I'll just stop before the timer goes off. I think I'm almost done anyway." It's these tiny moments, these split-second decisions, upon which your financial success rides. Not only do all these moments add up, but each one serves as a crack in your resolve where other excuses can, and will, seep in. Here's how to anchor in some nonnegotiating badassery:

a. Identify with the new habit. I'm a successful person who gets stuff done, not someone who screws around on Facebook. It's not even a blip on my radar. I don't drink, so why would I even consider taking a sip of alcohol any more than I would consider sniffing glue? I don't sniff glue and I don't drink. End of story.

b. Know thy negotiations. We tend not to be terribly creative or varied when we try to talk ourselves out of doing the stuff that's good for us. We tend to stick to the same script—if it ain't broke, don't fix it—so it should be easy to recognize your tried-and-true method for knocking yourself off track. Be on the lookout and the second your favorite excuse comes up—*Just one cigarette won't kill me* or *I'll just hit snooze and lie here for a few more minutes*—recognize the negotiation and do not consider it for even one tiny moment, because once you get into a conversation with it you're screwed. Just move along like it didn't even happen.

2. Connect your new habit to another habit or behavior. So many of our habits go hand in hand—drinking and smoking, exercising and eating well, lying, cheating, and stealing—that if you're trying to create a new habit, connecting it to an existing habit or behavior can really help. Let's say you want to get into the habit of being more focused. You could team this with shutting off your cell phone and putting it away. The physical act of dealing with the phone will trigger the mental reminder to focus on what's in front of you.

   Or let's say you want to get into the habit of taking risks. Maybe you come up with some sort of theme song that kicks into your head every time you're going to take a leap and do something scary. Or a cheering crowd. Or the sound of fireworks. Or maybe you start associating your morning cup of coffee with sitting down to read whatever motivational book you're reading. Create a buddy system for your new habit.

3. Strengthen your willpower. Along with staying emotionally attached to the Why of your goal, your willpower muscle can be strengthened by:

   a. Anticipating the discomfort. When you know doubling your rates is going to feel freaky and scary, feel into these feelings before bringing your new rates to your clients. Hang out in discomfort, get used to it, realize it's just part of the process and don't create a huge drama around it. Associate your discomfort with the awesomeness of moving forward and kicking ass instead of with something terrifying that can stop you.

   b. Find an accountability partner. We're all so much more likely to be on time, prepared, dressed in something other than our bathrobes when other people are involved. Find someone who's working to become a bigger badass like you are and ask them to be your accountability partner. Tell each other your goals each week and check in with each other periodically to make sure you're both staying on track. Remember, you've got to be cruel to be kind, so if your buddy says she's going to do something, don't let her off the hook, and ask her to do the same for you.

   c. Envision the end result with tearful giddiness. Before you even start what you're doing, get so excited that it's not only done, but that you totally knocked it out of the park. Feel the relief, the joy, the badassery first, and then get to work.

## COURSE CORRECT

Many years ago when I was in Milwaukee visiting a pal, we took a tour of the Miller Brewing Company. As we toured the facility, sipping samples of beer out of plastic cups, I was ensmartened about something I did not know and that gave me a newfound respect for the champagne of beers. Some sixty years after Miller Brewing opened its doors, the giant buzzkill of Prohibition swept the nation, ruining countless parties and devastating hundreds of breweries. But not Miller. Instead of being like, *Whelp, that was a fun, long run, should we see if the coffee shop down the street is still hiring?* they knew that when one door closes, another opens, and they looked for new ways to expand. They started producing malted milk, malt syrups, soda, and nonalcoholic beer, changed their name to Miller Products Co., and clung to life during a supershaky time. With these new products and some wise investments the family who owned the business had made, they managed to crawl through the dry, desert years until they made their way to the raging party on the other side of Prohibition.

They were a company that sold alcohol. Alcohol became illegal. They had three choices: break the law, admit defeat, or course correct. All you need to know is that if you desire something, it is available to you. Keeping that desire alive and more real than all the "signs" that it's time to throw in the towel eventually leads to success. Remember, it's not your job to know How, that's up to Universal Intelligence. Surrender is such a vital part of being tenacious—tenacity is not about pushing so hard you push away the very thing you're trying to achieve, it's about determined action paired with availability for the new, previously untaken paths that lead you where you desire to go. Staying the course involves some bends in the road. Being stubborn, refusing to go with the flow, will leave you in a ditch with an airbag exploded in your face. Never give up, course correct when necessary, and have faith that if you have the desire, the Universe has your back.

## TO GET RICH

Suggested Money Mantra (say it, write it, feel it, own it):
   *I love money and will not give up until I am surrounded by all the wealth I desire.*

1. Read the biography of someone who's rich and inspiring to you.

2. Notice three not-so-great habits that you've got and put together a plan to change them to good habits.

3. Go to the spiritual gym every day. What will you do every day to keep your frequency high, your faith strong, your mindset solid, and your tenacity unshakable? What self-help

book will you read, what music will you listen to to pump yourself up, what affirmations will you write, will you meditate, listen to meditations, journal, exercise? Put together some sort of spiritual practice that you will do every single solitary day to stay in shape. Even if it's just fifteen minutes a day, this is critical to your success. Mindset is a muscle, and just like your other muscles, once you get in shape you don't get to stop working out, you have to stay on it if you want to stay mighty.

Please fill in the blank:

I'm grateful to money because _____.

# CHAPTER 13

# CHANGE LOVES COMPANY

**M**y entire family lives within driving distance of the town I grew up in, and the last time I visited them, my brother and I decided to take a stroll down memory lane. We walked along the dirt trail that runs through the woods surrounding our old hood, turned down the street we lived on for the duration of our childhoods, and stood at the bottom of our old driveway. We tried, unsuccessfully, to find the graves of the countless members of our long-ago deceased animal family, now buried beneath a thick carpet of pachysandra by the side of the road: Schmoo, Little Gus, Spooky, Happy, Bubbles, Phreen, Bathead, Mr. Squirrely Jones, to name a few.

We walked by the Roys' house, our old-people neighbors with the pool, who were unbelievably idiotic when it came to taking hints as they never once invited us over, no matter how long we stood pressed up against the fence separating our properties, bathing suits on, towels in hand, watching them swim. We headed through town, past the middle school where I got punched in the stomach and called "a fat jerk times infinity" by Ivan Scott for beating him at boxball, and back into the woods, heading toward the next town over where the trail eventually opened up and disappeared into the massive grounds of a castle. This castle was once the private home of some wealthy Founding Father–type people and it was now a museum of sorts. We used to go here all the time as kids on school field trips and get educated on the history of the place by folks dressed up in old-timey clothes. They'd show us how to do things like churn butter and put a wax seal on a letter and explain how they used leeches instead of aspirin. Back then, this castle seemed like the biggest, grandest, most colossally huge building in the world. But as my brother and I stood there, it seemed so . . . wimpy. In fact, everything on our walk that day seemed unbelievably dinky—our old house, the kickball field in our backyard, even the Roys' stupid pool was smaller. We marveled at this while we walked, all of it making perfect sense since we were so much smaller back then. But, come on, the castle too? We were okay with it looking a little smaller, but this was ridiculous, this was a damn castle, it had some grandiosity to live up to! Was there another wing that we didn't notice, perhaps? Maybe if we walk over this way we can see . . . no? We wandered around, searching the grounds, convinced that what we were standing in front of must have been the gatehouse. Or maybe the gift shop? It must be the gift shop. But after a while we realized that that was it, the gigantic castle of our youth in all of its Lilliputian glory.

This is how it is when you grow in the mindset department

as well—so many things that once loomed large loom large no more. For example, think about something that was an all-consuming, gigantic fear that you conquered and that's now a mere pipsqueak of a memory, if you can even remember it at all: your first day at a new job, having your first kid, asking your spouse for a divorce, demanding a raise from your boss, that one time in high school when you took your parents' car without permission and had to tell them you accidentally drove it through the supermarket window when you lost control doing donuts in the parking lot. At the time, the discomfort was so intense you thought you might explode, and now when you think back on these fears, they just feel sort of meh.

As you evolve, it's helpful to keep in mind that all the seemingly insurmountable roadblocks and fears you're facing right now on your path to riches will be insignificant crumbs falling through the cracks of your memory someday too: your fear that focusing on making money will be a fun-free slog, your doubt that you could honestly ever get rich anyway, your worries about what others might think, your terror of taking the risks you need to take, your general feelings of overwhelm and self-suckery. Instead of getting caught up in the drama, see these limiting beliefs for what they are *as you're experiencing them*—they are make-believe. Imagine looking back upon them from the future when you're rollin' in the cheddah. In the future, you know for a fact that these unhelpful thoughts and beliefs are not the truth, that you possess the mighty mindset to disempower them, and that they have some serious shrinkage in store for them.

I remember back in the day, when I was diligently

working on my rickety relationship with money, I had a hard time believing all the whoop-de-do about mindset. All the screaming and yelling about positive thinking and faith and gratitude and awareness—seriously, there had to be more to getting rich than that. I imagined the process of overhauling one's financial situation to be more of a Rubik's Cubey–type challenge, or at least the grueling equivalent of going to graduate school or climbing a mountain with a large, clingy child on your back. But to learn that an unwavering decision to get rich—a decision, of all things!—was pretty much the main difference between my broke ass and all those people living large and in charge? *What do you take me for, a sucker?*

........................................................

Nature makes it easy, we make it hard.

........................................................

Of course, there are usually tenacious, terrifying, and radical leaps into the unknown involved in getting rich, but the big transformation truly does happen between your ears. And I want to stress that *it's not hard.* I can almost guarantee you that you've worked harder at other things in your life than you'll need to work to become a financial badass. I'm not saying you won't have to work hard at all, but I am saying that my life with money is a hell of a lot easier than my life without it ever was.

And here's the awesome bonus prize with this mastering your mindset thing, as if getting rich isn't awesome enough: Once you start shifting your mindset and getting into the flow with money, your energy will shift and many other parts of your life will start shifting too. When you transform your financial reality, it's not just about gleefully watching the numbers grow in your bank account, it's about who you had to become to make that growth happen. You had to shed your old ways of being, and grow into someone who thinks big, someone who finds possibility more interesting than you find your excuses, someone who regards your empty wallet, flimsy résumé, and zero idea of how the hell you're going to pull this off as cute little hiccups on your path to greatness. If you can get rich, you can do anything, because not only are you the kind of person who now kicks ass and takes names, but it's all connected. The limiting beliefs that held you back from making money are much of the same crap that's keeping that twenty pounds on or that inspires you to date people who don't like you or that has you clouded by doubt and indecision—the dam has been broken, the floodgates of bad-assery are now open, and your limiting beliefs have been exposed as the frauds they are.

It's like when you get in shape after a serious bout of lazy slobbiness, you start eating better, you walk taller, you're more focused, happier, more confident, more energized, more flirty, more well shaven. If you want to change your life, change your life.

........................................................

Badassery seeks its own level.

........................................................

I'd like to end here by reminding you that you not only have every single thing you need to get rich inside of you right now, but you've got the Universe backing you up and cheering you on, just as it does for every other living thing in nature. It's like when you see a friend who's so awesome and gorgeous and talented and she sits around worrying that she doesn't know what she's doing, doubting her brilliance, complaining about her weak chin—you want to shake her, wake her up, create a PowerPoint presentation highlighting all her awesome traits. You're so excited to show her her greatness and lovability, you so badly want her to understand that she could easily do whatever she set her mind to. You want her to see in herself what you see in her. This is how the Universe feels about you and your struggle with money. The Universe is having a heart attack thinking about how awesome you are, and it's got everything you need at the ready to help you get rich, it's just waiting for you to get out of your own way, stop focusing on your limiting beliefs, and get on the money party train.

We live in an abundant Universe where all the money you desire is available to you. As soon as you decide, really truly decide, to get rich, you open yourself up to the means to make it happen. Imagine how freaking awesome it's going to feel when you beat this beast of financial struggle into the ground? When you defy a lifetime's worth of "truths" about your ability to succeed, your worthiness, money's evil ways? Imagine the relief and feeling of accomplishment when you and money are BFFs, coming and going in each other's lives, happily supporting each other, braiding each other's hair. You've done the impossible before—you've gotten the job you were "unqualified" for, gotten the girl or the guy, moved across the country, bought the house, got the keys you locked in your car out without breaking a window. You can get rich too. You are mighty and magnificent beyond measure, grasshopper. You are meant to follow your desires. You are meant to blossom into the fullest expression of your unique and fantabulous badassery. You are meant to be rich.

# CHEAT SHEET:
# 10 WAYS TO SHIFT YOUR PERSPECTIVE AND CHANGE YOUR LIFE STARTING NOW

One of the most glorious powers we humans have is that we can radically change our realities simply by making the choice to adjust our focus.

Here is a cheat sheet of sorts, a meaty list of shortcuts that will empower you to overhaul your habitual way of looking at things, break you out of your rut (financial or otherwise), and become the Badass you were born to be.

### 1. Stay obsessed with your WHY

Radical change often comes down to simple reminders: Remember that you have but one shot at being the you that is you on planet Earth, that you've kicked ass before, and you can kick ass again. Remind yourself why you're excited to be, do, and have all that you're excited to be, do, and have. If you want to be successful, refuse to get hijacked by your doubts, fears, and worries by clinging like a barnacle to your Why. Why did you pick up this book in the first place? What excites you about making more money? How does it feel to picture yourself with the dream house, the passport full of stamps, the round of drinks you buy for everyone at the bar, the proof that you've just created the reality you decided to create? Walk around arm in arm with the you that you're becoming, wake up every morning remembering why you're excited to create what you're creating, take the time to visualize and feel yourself standing in your new reality, and you will give yourself the power to bulldoze past any negativity and stay the course to success.

## 2. Make fear your friend, not your foe

Poor fear. Fear gets such a bad rap. We blame it for so much that's wrong with our lives: "I'm going to stay in my hellhole of a job because I'm scared to lose the health insurance," "I'm scared if I raise my prices my clients will think I'm a greedy fathead, so I'll keep charging my measly fee and continue to be overworked, exhausted, and whiny," etc. Society has trained us to give fear all our power, to avoid feeling fear at all costs, to use fear as an excuse not to move forward. Meanwhile, when it comes to changing your life for the way better, fear is the secret ingredient you need to be a total badass. In order to change your life, you have to do things you've never done before, take risks, leap large, push yourself outside of your comfort zone, stretch and grow—all of which tend to be rather terrifying experiences for human beings. The sooner you start viewing fear as a sign that you're on the right track rather than as a sign to run screaming in the other direction, the sooner you'll start seeing results.

One of the most common questions I hear is "How do I

know if the fear I'm experiencing is a sign that I'm headed in the right direction or if my fear is warning me that I'm about to make a serious mistake?" Sometimes you don't know. Make the best choice you can, give it a shot, succeed or fail, learn from the experience, and keep going. Sitting around in tortured indecision is not an option. Also, get really good at tapping into your intuition if you want to better understand the fear you're feeling.

### 3. Respect your inner smartypants

There's a Zen proverb that goes something like this: *Sit in silent meditation for twenty minutes a day. Unless you are too busy, then sit for an hour.* Every moment of every day we choose between being swept away by the whirlwind of our lives or stepping back, breathing, and tapping into a deeper, more powerful knowing. We feel we don't have time to meditate because we have so much to do and figure out. Meanwhile if we made a practice of shutting up and sitting down for even ten minutes a day, the grocery shopping, the emails, the getting in shape, the impending "I deserve a raise" conversation with our boss, all of it would be much more manageable. Trust that you really do have all the answers inside of you, believe in yourself more than you believe in outward appearances and information, turn off your brain and listen to your intuition. Is the opportunity in front of you exciting? Does it feel right? Does it bring you joy? Our brains, as fabulous and impressive as they are, are cluttered with ideas of what we "should" do based on other people's opinions. Our brains are also rife with our own worries that we'll be judged or fail or get dumped, and all of this can lead us away from that which will make us truly happy. When we practice breathing deeply, slowing down, getting quiet, and looking inward, we strengthen our natural ability to recognize our truths and empower ourselves to be the biggest badasses we can be.

## 4. Seek and ye shall find

If you're operating under the belief that making money is hard, that the economy sucks, that people are generally idiots, you will—consciously or unconsciously—look for and find endless proof that you are correct. Humans, you see, love to be right. We get into habits of thinking, believing, and speaking about our "realities" in ways that create and perpetuate the reality we forget we've *chosen* to participate in. Should we decide we no longer want to have a hard time making money or feel horrible about the economy or be subject to countless idiots, the beautifully simple shift we must make is to seek out proof that the opposite is true. Find people who have jobs they enjoy, that are fun and easy and lucrative, and imagine yourself feeling that way about what you do for a living too. Look for ways that the economy is kicking ass, see that people are succeeding all over the place, and imagine yourself as a thriving contributor. Notice the brilliance in people, even the guy on the freeway who's all over the road because he's texting, be grateful that he's safely making his way through traffic instead of spending your energy crowning him King of the Morons. Every single moment offers countless opportunities to recognize and embrace gratitude as well as reasons to bitch and moan, and you have the glorious opportunity to choose which you will allow to shape your reality.

## 5. See through new eyes

Have you ever noticed how much easier it is to solve other people's problems than it is to solve your own? How deftly you can tell your pal Sally exactly how she needs to give Brad, who's loved her since high school, a chance even though she thinks his lips are too skinny, how she should ditch her goal of being a doctor because she hates medicine and is only doing it to please her parents and how, if she finally opened the bed and breakfast she's been talking about forever, she'd be a screaming success? Meanwhile, it takes you thirty minutes to decide what color to paint your nails and you've been bartending since college because you can't figure out what the hell to do with your life. We get so tangled up in the details of our own circumstances and bogged down by the what-ifs and why-nots that we can't see all the awesomeness we're capable of. Because we often can't see the forest for the trees, stepping back and getting a fresh perspective is incredibly helpful. One of my favorite exercises is to pretend you're an alien who's just landed on earth. As the alien, you observe your earthly self, seeing all of your talents, connections, brilliant ideas, opportunities, excitement, and possibilities, and you're oblivious to the baggage and insecurities and fears you're lugging around. Look at yourself from above and what do you see? List all the things that light you up, all the people who can help you, all the things you're awesome at, all the resources you have, all the reasons you're so irresistibly lovable, all your accomplishments, excellent personality traits, and perfect choices in nail colors. View yourself and your world minus the baggage and it's much easier to see the greatness that surrounds you and is you.

## 6. Intend

Instead of waking up and going about your life, doop de doo, taking out the trash, going off to work, meeting Helen for lunch, start each day by setting an intention. Snap out of your zone of regularity and take the helm instead of just rolling with the punches. Today I intend to do one thing that scares the crap out of me. Today I intend to smile at more people. Today I intend to breathe deeply as often as possible. Today I intend to speak nicely about everyone, including myself and my blowhard boss. Today I intend to do something I've never done before. Setting your intention puts you in the power seat because you train your focus on what you desire, acknowledge that you deserve it, set your thoughts, beliefs and actions in motion to manifest it, feel grateful that it's totally possible and happening, and become the agent of your own changes instead of being victim to your circumstances. It takes mere minutes and could open up entire new worlds for you.

## 7. Ask for help

If you fell down the stairs and landed on your face, you would go to a dental professional to replace the teeth you later found under your coffee table. We have no trouble seeking help in some areas of our lives, but we'll spend years, decades, maybe even lifetimes refusing to get help in other areas that are also causing us some serious suffering. Take, oh, myself for example. I spent the majority of my adult life scraping by, working my ass off for little pay with zero savings and all sorts of debt. And yet for decades I stubbornly insisted I would figure out how to get out of financial struggle on my own. I complained that I couldn't afford to get help, I didn't know who to ask for help anyway, and deep down I was too proud/ cool to get help. To make a much too long story short, when I finally could bear my brokenness no more and coughed up the money to get professional support, we quickly discovered where I was holding myself back financially, put a plan in place, got to work and for the first time I started making real money. If you're in a rut in a certain area of your life, instead of wasting extremely precious (and finite) time, figure out where you can go for help and get yourself some. A good coach or mentor or teacher can get you where you want to go in a fraction of the time you may take to get there on your own. Experienced, professional people can not only save you from making the same mistakes they made, provide you with resources, insight, accountability, guidance and belief in yourself, they also usually save you a buttload of money and time, the two things most people love to use as excuses *not* to get help. Also, please hang out with inspired, motivated, supportive people. We are so easily swayed into believing what the people around us believe that it's paramount to select our crew intentionally if we want to live an awesome life.

### 8. Use your words

Have you ever been riding a bike up a big hill or pulling an all nighter to finish a paper or attempting to please your Italian grandmother by eating all nine courses she puts in front of you? In these moments, you most likely have an inner dialogue running through your head: "I can do this, I can do this, I'm doing this, I will be triumphant." The moment you start negotiating with yourself, running through all the reasons you don't really need to get to the top of the hill or how you can maybe get an extension on your paper or how grandma is just going to have to deal with the disappointment of leftover meatballs, you are toast. You use words to psych yourself up and to psyche yourself out. We may not always be aware of their power, but words are like little whittling knives, carving our physical realities out of our thoughts. If you don't like what you see in your bank account or your love life or your mirror, notice the words you use to describe these "realities" and make the conscious choice to use words that reflect the outcome you'd love to see. "I'm a money magnet," "my soul mate is here and is looking for me too," "I am hot and sexy and on fire!" Regardless of how awkward it may feel at first, changing up your words will shift your focus away from building a case for the negative and bring in proof of the positive. Words also have the power to lift your energy and give you the strength and the attitude to push past your obstacles and create what you desire. When you upgrade your words, opportunities that you once talked yourself out of are suddenly full of thrilling possibility. We use words to communicate, and when you communicate optimism, inspiration and general badassery, you inspire other people and draw those who can help you toward you. Choosing your words wisely is one of the easiest and most powerful steps in changing your reality.

## 9. Show up for practice

Shifting the way you perceive your reality takes commitment and repetition; it's like strengthening a muscle or learning a new language or getting a cowlick to stay flat on your forehead. If you want to transform your life, make the conscious choice to read self-help books and anything else that inspires you; listen to music you love; exercise; get out in nature; hang out with brilliant, motivated people; educate yourself; get out of your comfort zone; meditate; stare at yourself in the mirror and tell yourself how fabulous you are. The key here is to be specific and consistent—figure out what makes you feel the most mighty and make a habit of doing those things. Maybe you meditate for twenty minutes, read for five minutes, and do forty sit-ups every morning. Whatever routine makes a notable difference in upping your confidence, your excitement, your connection to your intuition, your belief in what's possible for you, you're gonna want to make a nonnegotiable part of your day if you're serious about being a badass.

## 10. Be okay with the not okay

There is no such thing as perfect. To-do lists are never completed. Rain will fall on parades. You'll say stupid things, spill salsa on your shirt, and fail to remember where you put your phone over and over again. One of the greatest gifts you can give to yourself, and everyone within screaming distance of you, is the gift of letting it go. When we insist that flights should never be delayed or that people sitting next to us should not chew with their mouths open, we pull negativity and irritation into our focus when there's a whole wide world of positivity and good feelings available to us in that very same moment. I mean, feel all the feels, get upset, frustrated, sad, whatever. We are emotional creatures and we're not meant to bury our feelings—but lugging around negativity, bitching, regretting, hating, seething is . . . not exactly the best way to focus your energy. Make change where you can and accept, forgive and forget where you can't. Remember: Where you choose to place your attention dictates the reality you get to participate in. Choose to focus on the good instead of spending your one and only life stewing on the suckery.

# ACKNOWLEDGMENTS

This book wouldn't have happened without all the badasses who are out there bravely changing their lives and bettering the world. Thank you for believing in yourselves and for believing in me. Thanks to my agent, Peter Steinberg, for his many years of support, steady stream of great ideas, and quiet fierceness. Thanks to my editor and comrade in birth, Laura Tisdel, for her brilliant and hilarious insight, tireless cheerleading, and ability to think straight while nine-months pregnant. Thanks to Tami Abts, Juli Curtis, and Olive Curtis-Abts for taking care of Mokee and me. Thanks to the mighty crew at Viking: Lydia Hirt, Alison Klooster, Kristin Matzen, Jessica Miltenberger, Lindsay Prevette, Andrea Schultz, Kate Stark, Amy Sun, Brian Tart, Emily Wunderlich, Tess Espinoza, Jane Cavolina, and Jason Ramirez. Thanks to Downtown Subscription and my fellow regulars; all of the incredible booksellers who've helped spread the badassery; and my adorable friends and family who remind me on a daily basis how wealthy I truly am.